U.S. Tax Guides for Foreign Persons and Those Who Pay Them

U.S. Taxation of H-1B Specialty Workers

by Paula N. Singer

About the Author

Paula N. Singer, Esq., is a tax attorney and partner of the tax law firm, Vacovec, Mayotte & Singer LLP, located in Newton, Massachusetts, as well as co-founder and Chairman of the tax and immigration software company, Windstar Technologies, Inc.

Ms. Singer has advised individuals, businesses, and tax-exempt organizations on tax planning as well as provided compliance services for cross-border employee relocations, both inbound and outbound, since 1978. Ms. Singer is the author of a number of books and over 40 published articles appearing in such journals as Tax Analysts' *Tax Notes International*, West's *International HR Journal*, and the American Immigration Lawyers Association's annual *Immigration and Nationality Law Handbooks*. She has been a guest speaker on cross-border tax matters including treaties, for numerous tax and immigration law panels sponsored by trade organizations and software vendor groups.

In her capacity as a tax attorney, Ms. Singer has assisted the IRS with the development of key nonresident alien forms and regulations. She is chair of the American Bar Association Taxation Section international subcommittee, Individual Taxpayer Cross-Border Issues.

Ms. Singer began her tax career as a Tax Specialist at Peat Marwick following a ten-year career designing software in the insurance industry. She gained valuable immigration and international tax experience in her position as International HR Specialist at the international consulting firm, Arthur D. Little, Inc. where she was responsible for immigration processing and development of tax policies and procedures in support of the firm's relocating personnel.

Ms. Singer is a Phi Beta Kappa graduate of the University of Maine (Orono) and earned her JD degree at the University of Maine School of Law. A mother of two daughters, Beth and Samantha, and grandmother of twins, Grace and Rose, she resides in Massachusetts with her husband, Gary, and their dogs, Lilly and Callie.

This publication is designed to provide accurate information in regard to the subject matter covered. It is sold with the understanding that the publisher is not engaged in rendering legal, accounting or other professional services. If legal or other expert assistance is required, readers are advised to employ the services of a competent professional in such matters.

Published by Windstar Publishing

Copyright © 2001, 2002, 2003, 2005, 2006 Windstar Publishing, Inc.
P.O. Box 800, Norwood, MA 02062-0800

All rights reserved. Printed in the United States of America.
ISBN: 0-9769105-5-1

Distributed by
AILA Publications, *www.ailapubs.org*

Contents

Chapter 1: Introduction 1
   1.1 Work Authorization 1
   1.2 Taxpayer Identification Number 2

Chapter 2: U.S. Tax Residency Rules 5
   2.1 Residency Status Based on U.S. Presence 5
       (a) U.S. Days That Do Not Count 6
       (b) Closer Connection Exception 7
   2.2 Nonresidency Status Claims Based on an Income Tax Treaty 7

Chapter 3: Residency Start and Termination Dates 9
   3.1 Residency Start Date 9
       (a) The 10-day "de Minimis" Rule 9
       (b) Residency Start Date Under an Income Tax Treaty 10
   3.2 Tax Residency Elections 11
       (a) The First-year Choice Election 11
       (b) Full-year Residency Elections 13
   3.3 Residency Termination Date 14
       (a) Closer Connection Exception 14
       (b) Limitations Based on a Subsequent Year's Residency Status .. 15
       (c) Residency Termination Dates Under an Income Tax Treaty ... 17
       (d) H-1B Workers on Assignment Abroad 17

Chapter 4: Changes to H-1B Status 19
   4.1 Change of Status from J-1 Nonstudent to H-1B 19
   4.2 Changes from F-1 or J-1 Student Status 20

Chapter 5: Federal Income Tax Rules 23
   5.1 Tax Rules for Nonresidents 23
       (a) U.S. Source Income 23
       (b) Effectively Connected Income 24
   5.2 Tax Rules for Residents 25
       (a) Currency Translations 25
       (b) Sales of Assets Denominated in a Foreign Currency 26
       (c) Rental of Foreign Real Estate 26
       (d) Sale of a Principle Residence 26
       (e) Avoidance of Double Taxation 27
       (f) Disclosure of Foreign Financial Accounts 28
   5.3 Tax Rules for Dual-status Taxpayers 28
   5.4 Stock Ownership in a Foreign Corporation 28

Chapter 6: Income Tax Treaty Benefits 31
6.1 U.S. Source Income 31
6.2 Employment Compensation 32
    (a) Pre-Relocation Visits 32
    (b) Loss of Benefits 32
6.3 Compensation of Teachers and Researchers 33
    (a) Institution Where Teaching or Research Takes Place 34
    (b) Article Limitations 36
    (c) Successive Treaty Article Claims 39
    (d) Combined Benefit Periods 40
    (e) Back-to-back Limitations 40
6.4 Special Considerations for Research Scholars 41
    (a) Compensation for Services vs. Scholarship or Fellowship 41
    (b) Public Benefit Requirement 41

Chapter 7: State Income Taxes 43
7.1 Domicile 44
7.2 Residence 44
7.3 State Tax Rules 44
7.4 Income Tax Treaty Exemptions 44

Chapter 8: Withholding and Reporting 47
8.1 Benefits in Kind 47
    (a) Temporarily-Away-From-Home vs. Relocation 47
    (b) Tax Home 48
    (c) Temporarily Away-From-Home Expenses 49
    (d) Per Diems 49
    (e) Company-Provided Automobiles 50
    (f) Moving Expenses 51
    (g) Pension Plan Contributions 52
    (h) Tax Return Preparation Fees 52
    (i) Immigration Fees 53
8.2 Special Withholding Rules for Nonresidents 53
    (a) Residency Change Year 54
    (b) Full-year Residency Elections 55
8.3 Treaty Exempt Compensation 55
    (a) Form 8233 for Nonresident Treaty Claims 55
    (b) Form W-9 for Residents' Treaty Claims 56
    (c) Taxpayer Identification Number Requirement 57
    (d) Form 1042 and 1042-S Requirements 57
    (e) Coordination with Form W-2 Reporting 57
8.4 Social Security and Medicare Taxes 58
    (a) No Internal Revenue Code Exemption 58

(b) Exemption from Tax under a Social Security Agreement 59
(c) Exemption from Tax under an Income Tax Treaty 61
8.5 State Income Taxes 61

Chapter 9: U.S. Tax Returns 63
9.1 Sailing Permit Requirement 63
9.2 Federal Tax Return 64
    (a) Nonresident Tax Return 64
    (b) Resident Tax Return 64
    (c) Dual Status Tax Return 65
9.3 Treaty Claims 66
    (a) Nonresidents 67
    (b) Dual Residents 67
9.4 State Tax Returns 68

Chapter 10: Individual Taxpayer Identification Numbers 69
10.1 Individuals Eligible for ITINs 69
10.2 Documentation Requirements 70
10.3 Application Submission Procedures 71
    (a) Submissions with Tax Returns 71
    (b) Tax Return Extensions 72
    (c) Exceptions to the Tax Return Submission Procedures 73
10.4 Acceptance Agents 73
10.5 Acceptance Agent Application Procedures 74

Chapter 11: Resources 75
11.1 Websites 75
    The Internal Revenue Service (IRS) Website 75
    The Social Security Administration (SSA) 75
    Windstar Technologies, Inc. (Windstar) 75
11.2 IRS Publications 77
    Publication 15, *Circular E, Employer's Tax Guide* 77
    Publication 463, *Travel, Entertainment, Gift, and Car Expenses* 77
    Publication 515, *Withholding of Tax on Nonresident Aliens and Foreign Entities* 77
    Publication 517, *Moving Expenses* 78
    Publication 519, *U.S. Tax Guide for Aliens* 78
    Publication 901, *U.S. Tax Treaties* 78
    Other Helpful Publications 79

Index 81

CHAPTER 1
Introduction

The H-1B nonimmigrant category provides an opportunity for "specialty workers" to accept employment in the United States. H-1B Specialty Worker status must be obtained through petition to U.S. Citizenship and Immigration Service (referred to hereafter as the "immigration service") by U.S. employers or by foreign employers licensed to do business in the United States. H-1B Specialty Worker status may be granted for an initial period of up to three years. The status, which does not require a foreign residence, allows H-1B Workers to fill permanent positions as long as they are in that status. Once the status ends, H-1B Workers must depart the United States unless proper steps have been taken to change to a new status or adjust to U.S. lawful permanent residency status. H-1B status can be extended to up to six years with additional extensions available for certain specified situations. Employers must request extensions prior to the expiration of the H-1B Worker status.

1.1 Work Authorization

H-1B Specialty Workers are not permitted to work for any employers in the United States other than the one for which the immigration service approved the H-1B. Two issues are common for H-1B Workers in academia, 1) the type of payment being made by the sponsoring employer and 2) payment for speeches and lectures by non-sponsoring institutions. The H-1B Worker regulations make it clear that there is an employee-employer relationship between H-1B Workers and their sponsor. Therefore, payments made to H-1B Workers by their sponsors are in the nature of wages, not fellowships.

H-1B Workers may be invited to speak or give lectures at educational institutions. Based on a U.S. Department of Justice advisory opinion, H-1B workers in academia may give speeches, lectures, etc. at institutions other than their sponsoring institution as long as the activities are incidental to the workers' H-1B employment. For example, speaking on a panel at a conference in which the audience is the primary beneficiary of the activity would be permissible. In such situations, H-1B Workers may not derive monetary or other material gain from the activity, but may be provided with transportation and other incidental living expenses. However, when the primary beneficiary of H-1B Workers' activities is the nonsponsoring institution, which is the case when H-1B Workers teach classes, the activity is not permitted. In such situations, the nonsponsoring institution may pay the sponsoring institution for the H-1B Workers' activities provided that the activities are incidental to their employment with the sponsoring institution.

It is possible for an H-1B Worker to be employed by more than one employer concurrently. In that case, each employer must submit the appropriate petition. In order to change to a new employer, the new employer must submit a petition for H-1B Specialty Worker status for the employee. An H-1B Worker may work for a new employer upon the filing of the new petition without waiting for the notice of approval. An H-1B Worker for whom an application for extension has been timely submitted may continue to work for 240 days while the application for extension is being processed by the immigration service. If an application is denied, the employer may no longer employ the H-1B Worker.

For work authorization purposes, H-1B Workers must present to their U.S. employers the documentation listed on Form I-9, *Employment Verification Form*, List A #4 (an unexpired foreign passport and Form I-94, *Arrival/Departure Record*). Form I-9 is stamped with the H-1B classification and the approved H-1B admission period.

A spouse and minor children of H-1B Workers are in H-4 derivative status. Although dependents may not accept U.S. employment while in H-4 status, they may engage in full- or part-time study. Dependents in H-4 status may change status to any classification for which they are qualified in order to engage in other approved activities.

1.2 Taxpayer Identification Number

H-1B Specialty Workers are eligible to obtain U.S. Social Security numbers (SSNs) to be used by their U.S. employer to submit Form W-2, *Wage Reports*. Wage withholding and wage reports are required even if a foreign employer pays the remuneration for employees performing employment services for a U.S. employer. In most cases, H-1B Workers' SSN cards will bear the annotation "valid for work only with DHS authorization."

If issuance of an SSN is delayed, employers must nevertheless pay employees who have performed services in order to comply with U.S. labor laws. No SSN is required to pay a worker. However, federal income tax withholding in such cases must be based on single status and no exemptions until the SSN is received. If the payroll system requires an SSN, employers must use a temporary number which should not be included on a Form W-2. If no SSN has been received by the date for issuing Form W-2, the SSN on a paper copy should indicate "Applied For" and an electronic copy should be all zeroes. Employers must correct the Form W-2 when the SSN is finally received.

Accompanying H-4 dependents are not authorized to work and, therefore, are not eligible to obtain SSN cards. H-4 dependents may be able to obtain an Individual Taxpayer Identification Number (ITIN). This number is required for U.S. tax return purposes, such as for being claimed as a dependent for a personal exemption on a return. H-4 dependents obtain an ITIN by submitting a completed Form W-7, *Application for IRS Individual Taxpayer Identification Number*, with required documentation to the IRS.

For more information on obtaining an ITIN, refer to Chapter 10, "Individual Taxpayer Identification Numbers." Also refer to Chapter 11, "Resources" for where to find more information about ITIN applications.

CHAPTER 2
U.S. Tax Residency Rules

The federal income taxes of H-1B Workers depend on whether they are a *nonresident alien*, *resident alien* (hereafter *Nonresident* and *Resident*, respectively), or a Dual-status Taxpayers for the calendar year. Foreign nationals who are Residents are subject to tax in the same manner as U.S. Citizens. Foreign nationals who are Nonresidents are subject to tax under a completely different set of rules. Therefore, foreign nationals must first determine their U.S. tax residency status in order to determine the U.S. federal tax rules that apply to their income. (The U.S. tax rules for each residency status are explained in Chapter 5, "Federal Income Tax Rules.")

2.1 Residency Status Based on U.S. Presence

U.S. tax residency status of nonimmigrants, such as H-1B Workers, depends on their immigration category and substantial presence in the United States. Foreign nationals are Residents if they are substantially present in the United States over a period of years. Foreign nationals who are not substantially present are Nonresidents for tax purposes.

Foreign nationals are substantially present if their U.S. days (including partial days) over three consecutive calendar years equal or exceed 183 days based on a formula (called hereafter the "183-day residency formula"). Under this rule, foreign nationals who are present in the United States for 183 days or more in the calendar year are Residents unless an exception applies.

> **EXAMPLE** Sean, an H-1B Worker from Ireland, relocated to the United States in February 2005. Sean is a Resident in 2005 because his total days in the United States in 2005 exceed 183 days.

Foreign nationals who are not present in the United States for 183 days in the calendar year may nevertheless be Residents. Under the 183-day residency formula, foreign nationals who are in the United States for more than 30 days in the calendar year are Residents if they are substantially present based on a formula. The formula considers all their U.S. days in the current calendar year, plus one-third of their U.S. days in the prior calendar year, plus one-sixth of their U.S. days in the year before the prior year. Under this formula, foreign nationals who are in the United States fewer than 122 days per calendar year remain Nonresidents.

EXAMPLE 1 Dieter, an H-1B Worker from Germany, had been coming to the United States on business for a number of years for a different employer before relocating to the United States on July 20, 2005 to work for a new employer. He spent 165 days in the United States from his date of relocation not counting full days spent outside the United States on business during that period. He had 36 U.S. days in 2004 and 66 U.S. days in 2003. Under the 183-day residency formula, Dieter's U.S. days equal 188 (165 days plus 12 days plus 11 days). He is a Resident for 2005.

EXAMPLE 2 Glenn, an H-1B Specialty Worker from England, travels to and from the United States frequently. He is present in the United States for 121 days, including partial days, each year. Based on the formula, his U.S. days total $182\frac{1}{2}$ (121 in the current year, plus $40\frac{1}{3}$ [one-third of the prior year], plus $20\frac{1}{6}$ [one-sixth of the year before the prior year]). He remains a Nonresident.

Many foreign nationals change to H-1B Specialty Worker status from another immigration status such as F-1 Student, J-1 Student, or J-1 Nonstudent while in the United States. (Chapter 4, "Changes to H-1B Status" has examples of residency determinations for foreign nationals changing to H-1B Worker status from F-1 or J-1 status.) Foreign nationals may also enter the United States as H-1B Specialty Workers for employers that may be either affiliated with their home country employer or new employers.

Foreign nationals who become Residents must meet one of two exceptions, described in the following sections, to remain Nonresidents for the calendar year.

(a) U.S. Days That Do Not Count

For tax policy reasons, certain days have been excluded from counting for purposes of the 183-day residency formula. U.S. days that do not count include the following:

- Days spent regularly commuting to work in the United States from a residence in Canada or Mexico
- A day of less than 24 hours spent in the United States while in transit between two foreign locations
- Days spent when unable to leave the United States because of a medical condition that arose while in the United States (Form 8843 required)
- Days spent in the United States as a crewmember of a foreign vessel
- Days spent by a professional athlete engaged in a charitable event in the United States (Form 8843 required)
- Days spent in the United States as an "exempt individual" (that is, an individual exempt from counting U.S. days) (Form 8843 required)

(b) Closer Connection Exception

Foreign nationals who meet the 183-day test based on the formula but who are physically present in the United States for less than 183 days in the current year may be able to claim nonresidency status under the closer connection exception. In order to meet the closer connection exception, they must submit a completed Form 8840, *Closer Connection Statement for Aliens,* with facts supporting 1) a principal place of business for the full calendar year in a foreign country or countries and 2) a closer connection to a foreign country or countries than to the United States.

H-1B Workers who are on work assignments anticipated to last more than a year and have changed their tax homes to the United States are ineligible to claim this exception. H-1B Workers who travel to the United States in connection with short work assignments on a periodic basis but who do not relocate to the United States, may be able to use this exception if they otherwise meet the qualifying conditions.

Foreign nationals who have taken steps to become U.S. Lawful Permanent Residents cannot use the closer connection test to avoid U.S. tax residency status. These steps include the filing of government forms such as:

- Filings by the foreign national:
  - Form I-508, *Waiver of Immunities,* (waiver of closer ties to a foreign country by E and G aliens seeking adjustment of status)
  - Form I-485, *Application for Status of Permanent Resident*
  - Form DS-230, *Application for Immigrant Visa and Alien Registration* (filed at a U.S. consulate)
- Filings on behalf of the foreign national:
  - Form I-130, *Petition of Alien Relative*
  - Form I-140, *Petition for Prospective Immigrant Employee*
  - Form ETA-750, *Application for Alien Employment Certification*
  - Form ETA-9089, *Application for Permanent Employment Certification*

2.2 Nonresidency Status Claims Based on an Income Tax Treaty

The United States has income tax treaties in force with over 60 countries. Foreign nationals who are tax resident in a treaty country may be able to support a claim of nonresidency under the Residency Article of the applicable treaty. The Residency Article of most treaties includes a tie-breaker rule with a hierarchy of criteria, typically: permanent home, center of vital economic interests, habitual abode, and nationality. The criteria and sequence varies by treaty.

A permanent home can be a house, apartment, or rented furnished room that has been retained for permanent use by the foreign national. The center of vital economic interests considers a foreign national's family and social relations; occupation and place of business; political, cultural, or other activities; the place from which a foreign national administers property; etc. If a foreign national has a permanent home in both countries and the center of vital economic interests cannot be determined, the foreign national is resident in the country of habitual abode. This is the location where the foreign national spends more time. If none of these criteria are determinative, a foreign national is resident in the country of nationality.

Many H-1B Workers are no longer a tax resident in their home country following relocation to the United States and cannot use a tax treaty to reduce their U.S. income taxes. However, the treaty exception may be used to maintain U.S. nonresidency status up to either the date of relocation to the United States or the last day of tax residency in the treaty country, whichever is earlier. The nonresidency claim allows H-1B Workers to avoid being taxed on worldwide income prior to relocating to the United States. This exception may also be used by H-1B Workers who travel to the United States in connection with short work assignments on a periodic basis, but who do not relocate to the United States to avoid being taxed by the United States on worldwide income.

To claim nonresidency status under a tax treaty tie-breaker rule, taxpayers must attach to their tax returns a statement or Form 8833, *Treaty Based Disclosure Statement*, which includes the following information:

- A statement as to tax residency in the tax treaty country and the income tax treaty article number for the residency tie-breaker rule
- The U.S. code provisions that are overridden by the treaty, in this case Section 7701(b)
- The facts supporting a nonresidency status claim under the tie-breaker rule
- The period of time in the calendar year that the foreign national claims nonresidency status under the residency tie-breaker rule

(Refer to Chapter 11, "Resources" for websites with income tax treaties.)

CHAPTER 3
Residency Start and Termination Dates

Special rules determine the date that foreign nationals become Residents (called the "residency start date") and end U.S. tax residency (called the "residency termination date"). The residency start date and residency termination date may be changed by the tie-breaker rule of an income tax treaty in a foreign national's year of arrival in and/or year of departure from the United States.

3.1 Residency Start Date

Foreign nationals who become Residents in the calendar year and who were not Residents at any time during the preceding calendar year are Residents from their first day of physical presence in the United States in the calendar year. An exception may apply to make the residency start date a later date in the calendar year.

(a) The 10-day "de Minimis" Rule

Under the 10-day "de minimis" rule, Residents can ignore up to ten days of U.S. presence in determining the residency start date if they can establish that on those days they had 1) a closer connection to a foreign country than to the United States and 2) a tax home in that foreign country. Days from more than one period can be ignored as long as the days for the combined periods do not exceed ten days. Days cannot be ignored if all of the days in the consecutive period cannot be ignored.

> **EXAMPLE 1** Jeremy, a citizen and resident of the U.K., relocated to the United States as an H-1B Specialty Worker on April 1, 2005 and became a Resident of the United States. He had visited the United States for a business visit for five days in February. Jeremy is able to establish that he had a closer connection and tax home in the U.K. until March 31, 2005. His residency start date is April 1, 2005.

> **EXAMPLE 2** Jane, a citizen and resident of the U.K., relocated to the United States as an H-1B Specialty Worker on April 1, 2005 and became a Resident of the United States. She had visited the United States for a business visit for five days in February and for six days in March beginning March 2, 2005. Jane is able to establish that she had a closer connection to and a tax home in the U.K. through March 31, 2005. She can ignore the days from the first visit in determining only her residency start date because the combined days from the two visits exceed ten days. Therefore, her residency start date is March 2, 2005.

Note: The days that can be ignored for purposes of the residency start date still count in determining tax residency under the 183-day residency formula.

Arriving Residents may establish later residency start dates by attaching a statement to their tax return giving the facts supporting a later residency start date. The statement must contain the following information as applicable:

- Name, address, U.S. taxpayer identification number, and U.S. visa number (if any)
- Country issuing the passport and passport number
- The tax year for which the statement applies
- The last day that the taxpayer was present in the United States during the year
- U.S. days that are being ignored under the "de minimis" rule, if any
- Sufficient facts to show that the taxpayer's tax home is in a foreign country and that the taxpayer has a closer connection to that country than to the United States in the period prior to the claimed residency start date

The statement must be dated and signed under the penalties of perjury.

(b) Residency Start Date Under an Income Tax Treaty

Foreign nationals who are tax residents in a country that has an income tax treaty with the United States may be able to use the tie-breaker rule in the Residency Article to establish a later residency start date.

> **EXAMPLE** Peter, a citizen and resident of the U.K., relocated to the United States as an H-1B Worker on April 1, 2005 and became a Resident of the United States. He had visited the United States for a business visit for five days in February and for six days in March beginning March 2, 2005. Peter is able to establish that he had a closer connection and tax home in the U.K. until March 31, 2005. His residency start date is March 2, 2005 because the combined days from the two visits exceed ten days. However, Peter is able to establish under the tie-breaker rule of Article 4 of the U.S./U.K. income tax treaty that he was a resident of the U.K. and a NonResident of the U.S. through March 31. Therefore, his residency start date is April 1, 2005.

To claim nonresidency status under a tax treaty tie-breaker rule, taxpayers attach to their tax return a statement or Form 8833, *Treaty Based Disclosure Statement*, which includes the following information:

- A statement as to tax residency in the tax treaty country and the income tax treaty article number for the residency tie-breaker rule

- The U.S. code provisions that are overridden by the treaty, in this case Section 7701(b)
- The facts supporting a nonresidency status claim under the tie-breaker rule
- The period of time in the calendar year that the foreign national claims nonresidency status under the residency tie-breaker rule

(See Chapter 11, "Resources" for where to find more information about tax treaties.)

3.2 Tax Residency Elections

Foreign nationals whose U.S. presence does not meet the 183-day requirement for residency are Nonresidents for the calendar year. Foreign nationals who were not physically present in the United States on January 1 of the calendar year and who become Residents during that calendar year are Dual-status Taxpayers; i.e., part-year Nonresidents and part-year Residents for federal income tax purposes. U.S. tax rules for married Nonresidents and Dual-status Taxpayers (described in Chapter 5, "Federal Income Tax Rules") limit income and deductions. Foreign nationals' U.S. taxes may be lowered by making one or more of the following elections.

(a) The First-year Choice Election

Foreign nationals who are Nonresidents in the calendar year under the 183-day residency formula and who become Residents in the subsequent calendar year may be able to choose to be treated as Residents for part of the year during which they are Nonresidents. This election is referred to as the "first-year choice election" because it can be made in the first year that foreign nationals relocate to the United States and fail to meet the 183-day residency formula until the subsequent calendar year. Foreign nationals typically make this election in order to claim personal exemptions for accompanying dependents and mortgage interest and real estate tax deductions related to residences in the United States or the home country or both.

To make this election, foreign nationals must 1) be physically present for a consecutive period of at least 31 days in the United States in the calendar year and 2) present in the United States for at least 75 percent of the days beginning with the first day in the 31-day consecutive period and ending on December 31 of the calendar year. For purposes of the 75-percent requirement, up to five days of absence from the United States may be ignored. When foreign nationals make this election, their residency start date is the first day of the earliest 31-day period that can be used to qualify for the election.

EXAMPLE 1 Francois, a citizen and resident of France, relocated to the United States as an H-1B Worker on November 1, 2004 and was present for 31 consecutive days through December 1, 2004. He returned to France for a business trip on December 1 and then returned on December 17 where he stayed for the remainder of the year. He became a Resident in 2005 under the 183-day residency formula. Francois can make the first-year choice election because he was present in the United States at least 75 percent of the days from November 1, 2004 through December 31, 2004. He had 46 days of presence out of 61 days for a total of 75.4 percent of the days.

EXAMPLE 2 Catherine, a citizen and resident of France, relocated to the United States as an H-1B Worker on November 1, 2004 under the same facts as the above example except that she returns to France for December 24–30. Catherine can still make the first-year choice election because up to five days of absence from the United States can be ignored for purposes of the 75-percent requirement.

First-year Choice Election Procedures

In order to make the first-year choice election, foreign nationals must attach a statement to their dual-status tax return that includes all the following information:

- Name and address of the electing foreign national
- A statement that the foreign national is making the first-year choice election
- A statement that the foreign national was not a Resident in the preceding calendar year and is a Resident in the subsequent year
- The number of days of presence in the subsequent year
- The dates of the 31-consecutive day period
- The dates of absence, if any, that are being ignored for purposes of the 75 percent requirement

Foreign nationals making this election cannot submit a tax return for the calendar year of the election until their U.S. presence has satisfied the 183-day residency formula in the subsequent calendar year. This may require a submission of an extension of time to file the current calendar year's tax return until the day on which they become Residents in the subsequent calendar year.

Election by Accompanying Dependents

Generally, in order to claim personal exemptions for accompanying dependents, the dependents must meet the qualifying criteria for dependency status and be either U.S. Citizens or Residents (unless one of the exceptions described in Chapter 5, "Federal Income Tax Rules," applies). Therefore, dependents who are nonresidents cannot be claimed for personal exemption purposes.

A first-year choice election can be made by an accompanying spouse and children who qualify for the election based on their respective days of U.S. presence. Foreign nationals who are eligible to make this election can claim their spouse and children who are U.S. Citizens or Residents as dependents for the personal exemption. Dependents with an ITIN who are eligible for this first-year choice election can be claimed as dependents on U.S. tax returns.

Because the first-year choice election cannot be made until foreign nationals have satisfied the 183-day residency formula in the subsequent calendar year, this election is not available for wage withholding purposes.

(b) Full-year Residency Elections

Married Nonresidents and Dual-status Taxpayers may be able make elections to be treated as Residents for the full calendar year. Nonresidents married to U.S. Citizens or Residents at the end of the year can make an election to be treated as a Resident for the entire calendar year. Married Nonresidents, who are Residents on December 31, may elect to be treated as Residents for the full calendar year. This election includes situations in which both foreign nationals are Nonresidents at the beginning of the calendar year and Residents at the end of the calendar year. The election also includes situations in which one spouse is a Nonresident at the beginning of the year but a Resident at the end of the calendar year, and the other spouse is a Nonresident at the end of the calendar year.

Election on a Tax Return

Married foreign nationals who make a full-year election must include worldwide income in their tax return and submit a joint return for the year of the election. Foreign nationals make this election when it results in a lower tax because of the more favorable deductions and graduated tax rates for joint tax returns. IRS Publication 519, *U.S. Tax Guide for Aliens*, explains how to make the election and the limitations on foreign nationals who have made an election. An election is terminated by death, divorce, or revocation or by the married Residents becoming Nonresidents following their departure from the United States.

Married foreign nationals who qualify for the first-year choice election may also make a full-year residency election based on their part-year residency status under the first-year choice election.

Wage-withholding Elections

Foreign nationals who expect to make the full-year residency election on their tax returns can also make the election for wage-withholding purposes. However, foreign nationals who are part-year Residents based on a first-year choice election can make the full-year election for tax return purposes only. Such foreign nationals cannot make the full-year election for wage-withholding purposes because all the events required to satisfy the first-year election will not occur until the subsequent calendar year.

3.3 Residency Termination Date

Foreign nationals who are Residents, and who later relocate from the United States, are deemed to be Residents through the end of the calendar of the year of departure. Foreign nationals who are not Residents for any part of the calendar year following the year of departure have a residency termination date of December 31 unless they qualify for an earlier residency termination date under one of the following exceptions.

(a) Closer Connection Exception

Departing Residents may establish an earlier residency termination date by showing that, during the period following their last day of physical presence in the United States, their tax home was in a foreign country and they maintained a closer connection to that foreign country than to the United States. Under the "de minimis" rule, foreign nationals may be in the United States for up to ten days following departure without changing their residency termination date from the date of departure. However, they may not disregard any days that occur in a period of consecutive days of presence if all the days that occur during that period cannot be excluded.

> **EXAMPLE** Sylvia departed the United States on August 15, 2005. She returns for a business visit of 12 days in 2005, five days in September and seven days in December. She can exclude the seven days in December but not the five days in September because the total exceeds ten days. Sylvia's residency termination date is her last day of U.S. presence in September. The business trip in December has the affect of extending her period of U.S. residency.

Note: Even though this foreign national can disregard the days for purposes of the residency termination date, the days count for purposes of the 183-day residency formula.

Departing Residents may establish earlier residency termination dates by attaching a statement to their tax returns giving the facts supporting an earlier termination date. The statement must contain the following information as applicable:

- Name, address, U.S. taxpayer identification number, and U.S. visa number (if any)
- Country issuing the passport and passport number
- The tax year for which the statement applies
- The last day that the taxpayer was present in the United States during the year
- U.S. days that are being ignored under the "de minimis" rule, if any

  The dates that are being ignored must be noted as well as sufficient facts showing that the taxpayers had a tax home in and a closer connection to a foreign country during the period that includes the "de minimis" days.

- Sufficient facts to show that the taxpayer's tax home has changed to a foreign country and that the taxpayer has a closer connection to that country than to the United States in the period following the claimed residency termination date

The statement must be dated and signed under the penalties of perjury.

(b) Limitations Based on a Subsequent Year's Residency Status

Foreign nationals who become Residents of the United States, and who returned home and later relocate to the United States and become Residents for tax purposes again, may cause a change in U.S. taxation in the intervening years.

The Consecutive Dual-status Year Rule

Foreign nationals who are Residents for part of a calendar year under the closer connection exception and who become Residents for part of the subsequent calendar year, are dual-status Residents for two consecutive years. Under the consecutive dual-status-year rule, they are treated as Residents for both full calendar years. Therefore, to remain part-year Nonresidents following departure from the United States, foreign nationals must have at least one full-calendar year as Nonresidents between calendar years as part-year Residents.

> **EXAMPLE 1** Jonathan, an H-1B Specialty Worker, departed the United States in October 2004 and filed a dual-status tax return as a part-year Resident and a part-year Nonresident using the closer connection exception. He relocated to the United States in E-1 status in August 2005 and became a part-year Resident under the 183-day residency formula. Jonathan is a Resident for all of 2004 and 2005.

> **EXAMPLE 2** Janice, an H-1B Specialty Worker, departed the United States in October 2003 and filed a dual-status tax return as a part-year Resident and a part-year Nonresident using the closer connection exception. She relocated to the United States in E-1 status in August 2005 and became a part-year Resident under the 183-day residency formula. She is a part-year Resident for both 2003 and 2005 and a Nonresident for 2004.

The Anti-Avoidance Rule

In addition to the above limitation, foreign nationals who, after having been Residents for at least three consecutive calendar years, become Residents in a subsequent calendar year may lose the favorable tax treatment accorded to Nonresidents on sales of U.S. securities (explained in Chapter 5, "Federal Tax Rules"). This tax rule is intended to prevent foreign nationals from departing the United States for relatively short periods to take advantage of the favorable tax treatment for such sales.

Under this rule, the exclusion for such sales by Nonresidents applies if the foreign nationals 1) were present in the United States for at least 183 days in each of the three consecutive calendar years as Residents and 2) were Nonresidents of the United States less than three full calendar years. In addition, for the rule to apply, the tax computed under the anti-avoidance rule must exceed the foreign nationals' U.S. tax computed under the normal rules for Nonresidents.

> **EXAMPLE** Miguel, an H-1B Specialty Worker, departed the United States in October 2003 and filed a part-year tax return using the closer connection exception. He had been a Resident of the United States for five calendar years during which time he was present in the United States for 183 days each year. He relocated to the United States in E-1 status in August 2005 and became a part-year Resident under the 183-day residency formula. Miguel is a part-year Resident for both 2003 and 2005 and a Nonresident for 2004. His only U.S. tax for 2003 is a small tax on dividends paid on his U.S. investment income. For 2004 his capital gains on sales of U.S. securities are subject to U.S. income tax at a 30-percent rate because this tax exceeds his U.S. tax as a Nonresident under the normal rules.

(c) Residency Termination Dates Under an Income Tax Treaty

Foreign nationals who, following their departure from the United States, become tax Residents of a country with which the United States has an income tax treaty may be able to claim an earlier residency termination date if the tax treaty includes a residency tie-breaker rule. Taxpayers can use the tie-breaker rule to claim nonresidency status for that part of the year in which the treaty rules result in nonresidency status. See the explanation of the residency tie-breaker rule in Chapter 2, "U.S. Tax Residency Rules.")

To claim nonresidency status under a tax treaty tie-breaker rule, taxpayers must attach a statement or Form 8833, *Treaty Based Disclosure Statement*, which includes the following information:

- A statement as to tax residency in the tax treaty country and the income tax treaty article number for the residency tie-breaker rule
- The U.S. code provisions that are overridden by the treaty, in this case Section 7701(b)
- The facts supporting a nonresidency status claim under the tie-breaker rule
- The period of time in the calendar year that the foreign national is claiming nonresidency status under the residency tie-breaker rule

(Refer to Chapter 11, "Resources" for where to find more information about tax treaties.)

(d) H-1B Workers on Assignment Abroad

It is not unusual for employers to send H-1B Workers abroad for temporary assignments. As a general rule, Nonresidents performing services outside the United States are not subject to U.S. income taxes on wages for such foreign services. However, in order for H-1B workers who have become Residents to become Nonresidents once again, they must terminate U.S. residency under one of the methods described above under Residency Termination Date. If they travel back to the United States periodically, they may remain Residents throughout the period of the overseas assignment.

Compensation for employment services performed outside the United States for an American employer by Nonresidents is not subject to U.S. Social Security and Medicare taxes. However, under a special deemed employee rule, the Social Security Administration will extend coverage to Nonresidents under a social security agreement if the Nonresident worker:

- Has been employed in the United States for at least six months and both the Nonresident worker and the employer paid Social Security taxes during this six-month period
- Has been assigned to a country that has a social security agreement with the United States
- Remains on the American payroll
- Remains under the managerial control of the American employer

The coverage will not extend to another country under that country's social security agreement with the United States without the Nonresident worker being first transferred back to the United States where the worker will be employed and contributing to U.S. Social Security for at least six months. (For more information on social security agreements, refer to Chapter 8, "Withholding and Reporting.")

Because these situations can be fraught with problems, employers planning to send H-1B Workers abroad for temporary assignments are advised to seek expert advice on how to plan the assignment.

CHAPTER 4
Changes to H-1B Status

The following foreign nationals may change status to H-1B Specialty Worker while in the United States:

- J-1 Nonstudents who are not subject to the two-year overseas residency requirement or obtain a waiver of such requirement
- F-1 Students
- J-1 Students

The U.S. tax status of foreign nationals during the transition depends on 1) the residency formula that applies to the new status and 2) whether or not the foreign nationals are exempt from counting U.S. days while in F-1 or J-1 status in the calendar year of the change.

4.1 Change of Status from J-1 Nonstudent to H-1B

Under the 183-day residency formula, J-1 Nonstudents do not count U.S. days for two out of the seven current calendar years. Any U.S. days from prior years as exempt individuals in F, M, J, or Q status must be considered in determining years in which U.S. days are countable under the special rules for J-1 Nonstudents.

J-1 Nonstudents who change to H-1B status must immediately begin counting U.S. days for purposes of the 183-day residency formula whether or not they were required to count U.S. days while in J-1 Nonstudent status. Their U.S. residency status in the calendar year of change depends on 1) whether or not they were counting U.S. days while in J-1 Nonstudent status and 2) the first day of H-1B status.

> **EXAMPLE 1** Vanessa is in her second calendar year in J-1 Nonstudent status and does not count her U.S. days for purposes of the 183-day residency formula. She has not been in the United States before her visit in J-1 status. She changes to H-1B status on September 1, 2005. Vanessa is a Nonresident for the full calendar year 2005 because her U.S. days while in J-1 Nonstudent status do not count and she has fewer than 183 U.S. days in H-1B status in 2005.

> **EXAMPLE 2** The same facts except that Vanessa changes to H-1B status on June 30, 2005. Vanessa is a part-year Nonresident from January 1 to June 29 and a part-year Resident from June 30 to December 31, 2005 because her U.S. days in H-1B status exceed 183 days.

EXAMPLE 3 The same facts except that Vanessa is in her third year in J-1 Nonstudent status and must count her U.S. days in that status for purposes of the 183-day residency formula. She changes to H-1B status on September 1, 2005. Vanessa is a Resident for the full calendar year 2005 because she must count both her U.S. days in J-1 Nonstudent status and her U.S. days in H-1B status. She has 365 countable U.S. days in 2005.

Example 4: The same facts except that Vanessa is in her third year in J-1 Nonstudent status and must count her U.S. days in that status for purposes of the 183-day residency formula. She changes to H-1B status on June 30, 2005. Vanessa is a Resident for the full calendar year 2005 because she must count both her U.S. days in J-1 Nonstudent status and her U.S. days in H-1B status. She has 365 countable U.S. days in 2005.

4.2 Changes from F-1 or J-1 Student Status

Under the 183-day residency formula, F-1 or J-1 students do not count U.S. days for five calendar years. Any prior calendar year in the United States in F, M, J, or Q status as an exempt individual (student or nonstudent) from and including 1985 counts toward these five calendar years.

F-1 and J-1 Students who change to H-1B status must immediately begin counting U.S. days for purposes of the 183-day residency formula whether or not they were required to count U.S. days while in F-1 or J-1 Student status. Their U.S. residency status in the calendar year of change depends on 1) whether or not they must count their U.S. days while in F-1 or J-1 Student status and 2) the first day in H-1B status.

EXAMPLE 1 Karen is in her second calendar year in F-1 Student status and does not count her U.S. days while in F-1 Student status for purposes of the 183-day residency formula. She had not been in the United States before her visit in F-1 status. She changes to H-1B status on September 1, 2005. Karen is a Nonresident for the full calendar year 2005 because her U.S. days while in F-1 Student status do not count and she has fewer than 183 U.S. days in the calendar year in H-1B status.

EXAMPLE 2 The same facts except that Karen changes to H-1B status on June 30, 2005. Karen is a part-year Nonresident from January 1 to June 29 and a part-year Resident from June 30 to December 31, 2005 because her U.S. days in H-1B status exceed 183 days.

EXAMPLE 3 The same facts except that Karen is in her sixth year in F-1 Student status and must count her U.S. days in that status for purposes of the 183-day residency formula. She changes to H-1B status on September 1, 2005. Karen is a Resident for the full calendar year 2004 because she must count both her U.S. days in F-1 Student status and her U.S. days in H-1B status. She has 365 countable U.S. days in 2005.

EXAMPLE 4 The same facts except that Karen is in her sixth year in F-1 Student status and must count her U.S. days in that status for purposes of the 183-day residency formula. She changes to H-1B status on June 30, 2005. Karen is a Resident for the full calendar year because she must count both her U.S. days in F-1 Student status and her U.S. days in H-1B status. She has 365 countable U.S. days in 2005.

Note: The analyses in these examples apply to changes to any U.S. immigration status in which the U.S. days count for purposes of the 183-day residency formula.

CHAPTER 5
Federal Income Tax Rules

The federal income taxes of H-1B Specialty Workers depend on whether the foreign nationals are Nonresidents, Residents, or Dual-status Taxpayers for the calendar year.

5.1 Tax Rules for Nonresidents

Foreign nationals who are a Nonresident under the 183-day residency formula, or under one its exceptions, are subject to U.S. tax only on income that is derived from or connected to the United States. How that income is taxed depends on whether the income is considered to be fixed or determinable, annual or periodic, or effectively connected to a U.S. trade or business. The tax rules explained below are discussed more fully in IRS Publications 519, *U.S. Tax Guide for Aliens*, and 515, *Withholding on Payments to Nonresidents and Foreign Entities*.

(a) U.S. Source Income

In general, the income of Nonresidents subject to U.S. tax may be in any one of four categories:

- Fixed or determinable, annual or periodical (called "FDAP") income that the taxpayer derived from sources within the United States where that income is not effectively connected to a U.S. trade or business

  This FDAP category, which includes but is not limited to rents, royalties, dividends, and interest, is subject to tax on gross income at a 30-percent rate or a lower tax treaty rate if available.

- Income or gain derived from U.S. sources that is not FDAP, but is similar to, and nevertheless taxed like, FDAP income

- Income that is, or is deemed to be, effectively connected with a U.S. trade or business (called "effectively connected income" or "ECI")

  This ECI income category is taxed on a net basis at graduated tax rates. This category includes compensation for personal services and the gain on sale of U.S. real estate. Some types of income that are taxed as ECI on a tax return, such as self-employment income, pensions, and certain scholarships and fellowships, are nevertheless subject to FDAP withholding.

- Capital gains derived from the sale or exchange of personal property that is not ECI

  This capital gain provision applies if the gain is sourced in the United States and the Nonresident recipient is physically present in the United States for at least 183 days during the year of the sale.

If the beneficial owner of U.S. income submits a signed and dated Form W-8BEN, *Certificate of Foreign Status*, with Part I completed to a withholding agent before the payment is made, the payment will be subject to 30-percent withholding or lower treaty rate, if applicable, and reported on Form 1042-S. If the beneficial owner of the income submits Form W-9 as a certificate of U.S. status and includes an SSN or ITIN, and the payer has no reason to know that the recipient is a Nonresident, the income is governed by the rules that apply to payments to U.S. Citizens and Residents.

Special tax rules apply to exclude the following income of Nonresidents from tax:

- Interest on deposits in U.S. banks, savings and loans, and insurance companies
- Portfolio interest on certain registered investments that meet specific conditions
- Capital gains on the sales of U.S. securities and debt obligations provided that the following two conditions are:
  - The foreign national's tax home is not in the United States at the time of the gain
  - The foreign national has *not* been physically present in the United States for 183 days or more in the calendar year of sale

Note: The 183-day gain exclusion rule is a different rule than the 183-day residency formula.

(b) Effectively Connected Income

Income effectively connected to a U.S. trade or business includes employment or self-employment compensation for services performed in the United States. The fact that the compensation is paid in a foreign currency or by a foreign employer does not change this rule. When services are performed both within and without the United States, the source of the compensation for regular pay is determined on a time basis. Compensation is apportioned between U.S. and foreign sources by multiplying total compensation by U.S. workdays over total workdays for the period for which the compensation is paid.

Chapter 5 • Federal Income Tax Rules

EXAMPLE Juan, an H-1B Worker, traveled to the United States periodically for services related to an affiliated company during 2005. He is a Nonresident of the United States under the 183-day residency formula for the calendar year. Juan's foreign employer pays his compensation. He had 96 U.S. workdays out of a total of 240 workdays in 2005. He is not a resident of a country with which the United States has an income tax treaty. Forty percent of Juan's compensation is for U.S. services and is subject to U.S. tax.

The source of income for employee fringe benefits with a geographical basis, such as company provided housing and moving expenses, is determined based on the principal place of work.

The gain on the sale of U.S. real estate by Nonresidents is treated as effectively connected income. The gross proceeds are subject to ten-percent withholding unless an exception applies and the seller submits appropriate paperwork at the closing.

Effectively connected income is subject to tax at single or married filing separately rates. Deductions from this income are allowed for state income taxes, business expenses, charitable contributions to U.S. charities, and casualty losses. Except for residents of certain countries, Nonresidents are entitled to one personal exemption.

5.2 Tax Rules for Residents

Foreign nationals who become U.S. Residents under the 183-day residency formula are subject to U.S. tax on worldwide income received, or constructively received, during the period of residence. With few exceptions, tax rules that apply to U.S. Citizens apply to Residents as well. Residents can claim deductions for worldwide expenses such as mortgage interest and real estate taxes paid on a personal residence including a residence in a foreign country. The following sections are some of the special rules that may apply in determining the U.S. tax of Residents.

(a) Currency Translations

All transactions involving assets denominated in a foreign currency must be translated into U.S. dollars using IRS rules. Compensation paid in a foreign currency is translated into U.S. dollars using the exchange rate of the currency to the U.S. dollar as of the date of the payment. If income is received evenly throughout the year, the currency can be translated to U.S. dollars using the average exchange rate for the period if the foreign exchange rate was relatively stable for the period.

A special IRS rule applies to sales of assets denominated in a foreign currency, such as foreign real estate or foreign securities. Under this rule (referred to hereafter as the "Quijano rule" for the taxpayer who challenged the rule on Constitutional grounds and lost), the basis in the property must be translated into U.S. dollars using the exchange rate as of the date of acquisition. The basis of property is the cost of the property plus the cost of acquiring the property. For inherited property, the basis is the fair market value on the date of death of the decedent. For property acquired by gift, the basis and date acquired are carried over from the donor. The proceeds from the sale must be translated into U.S. dollars using the exchange rate in effect on the date of sale.

(b) Sales of Assets Denominated in a Foreign Currency

Under the Quijano rule, the sale of an asset denominated in a foreign currency results in an unrealized exchange gain or loss being included in the net gain or loss on the sale. Depending on the change in the exchange rate between the two dates, a sale that results in an actual economic gain can result in a loss for U.S. tax purposes. A sale that results in an actual economic loss can result in a gain for U.S. tax purposes. Residents are advised to seek expert tax advice before selling assets denominated in a foreign currency to avoid unexpected U.S. taxes resulting from an unrealized exchange gain.

(c) Rental of Foreign Real Estate

The net income or loss on the rental of foreign real estate must be determined using U.S. tax rules and reported on a Form 1040 tax return on Schedule E. Depreciation on an asset located predominately outside the United States is computed over 40 years for real estate and 12 years for other depreciable property. The basis of the property for depreciation purposes is determined using the U.S. dollar exchange rate as of the date of acquisition of the property.

(d) Sale of a Principle Residence

The sale of a foreign principle residence is governed by the same U.S. tax rules that apply to the sale of a U.S. principle residence. The gain on the sale is translated into U.S. dollars using the Quijano rule. If the owner submits a joint tax return, the excludable gain for a qualified sale is $500,000. If the owner is single or is married but filing separately, up to $250,000 can be excluded. To qualify for the gain exclusion the residence must have been used as the principle residence for two out of five years prior to the date of sale. Residents who used the residence for less than the requisite period, but who moved for work-related reasons, may compute a pro-rata exclusion by multiplying the exclusion by the period of use divided by two years.

The Quijano rule also applies to the payoff of a foreign-denominated mortgage. The measure of the gain or loss is determined with reference to the exchange rate on the date that the mortgage was acquired and the exchange rate as of the date of payoff. If the payoff results in a gain, the gain is subject to U.S. tax. If the payoff results in a loss, the loss is disallowed because no losses are allowed for personal debts. (This rule, which is based on an IRS revenue ruling, is not explained in any IRS publications.)

(e) Avoidance of Double Taxation

Residents may also be paying foreign taxes on foreign transactions. Foreign transactions that result in income or gain under U.S. tax rules are subject to U.S. tax as well. In order to avoid double taxation, the U.S. allows a foreign tax credit to be claimed on a U.S. tax return. The tax credit is limited to the lesser of the available foreign taxes or U.S. taxes that are attributable to foreign income. The foreign tax credit can be claimed either on a cash or accrual basis. Using the accrual basis usually results in a higher credit since the foreign taxes are matched to the income on which the taxes are paid.

The credit is limited to foreign income taxes and taxes in lieu of income taxes, such as foreign social security taxes that are computed on income. However, Residents who are covered by a social security agreement, and therefore pay social security taxes to their home country, cannot use the home country social security taxes for foreign tax credit purposes.

Double taxation may be avoided by foreign tax credits but higher taxation is not. If a transaction is exempt from foreign tax, the transaction may nevertheless be subject to U.S. tax under U.S. tax rules. If the U.S. tax is lower than the foreign tax, Residents pay the higher foreign tax and receive a foreign tax credit at the lower U.S. tax rates.

Foreign tax credits are computed on Form 1116, *Foreign Tax Credit (Individual, Estate, or Trust)*, and submitted with a Resident's Form 1040 tax return. Foreign taxes not used can be carried backward and forward for a specified period of years. These foreign tax credit rules can be exceedingly complex when applied to individual transactions. Refer to IRS Publication 514, *Foreign Tax Credits*, for more information about these rules. As a practical matter, Residents eligible for foreign tax credits may wish to engage a tax return preparer knowledgeable in these rules and forms to prepare the tax return.

(f) Disclosure of Foreign Financial Accounts

Residents who have financial interests in, or signature authority over, foreign financial accounts must disclose the interest in the accounts if the aggregate value of the accounts exceeds $10,000 at any time during the calendar year. The financial accounts may be bank, securities, or other types of financial accounts in a foreign country.

Residents must disclose such foreign accounts as follows:

- By answering "yes" to the question posed about such accounts and indicating the country or countries where such accounts are held, at the bottom of Schedule B, *Interest and Ordinary Dividends*, of the Form 1040 tax return
- By submitting Form TD 90-22.1, *Report of Foreign Bank and Financial Accounts*, to the IRS by June 30 of the subsequent calendar year

5.3 Tax Rules for Dual-status Taxpayers

Foreign nationals who are part-year Residents, either in the year of arrival in or departure from the United States, determine income and deductions with reference to the tax rules for the respective nonresidency and residency periods in the calendar year. Income and expenses paid in the residency period are governed by the rules that apply to U.S. Citizens and Residents with some limitations. For example, Dual-status Taxpayers cannot claim the standard deduction, and married Dual-status Taxpayers cannot file jointly. Income and expenses paid during the nonresidency period are governed by the tax rules for Nonresidents.

(Refer to Chapter 9, "U.S. Tax Returns" for more information on dual-status tax returns.)

5.4 Stock Ownership in a Foreign Corporation

Income earned in foreign corporations from foreign operations is generally subject to U.S. tax when the income is distributed to U.S. Citizens and Residents who hold stock in the corporations. The foreign nationals must report the income in their U.S. tax return in the year in which distributions are received. A foreign tax credit may be available to reduce the U.S. tax imposed on the distribution.

However, income earned in certain foreign corporations may be taxed currently to U.S. Residents who hold stock in the corporations *even if the income is not distributed out of the corporations to the stockholders*. These rules are designed to prevent U.S. persons from placing passive investment assets in off-shore companies to avoid U.S. income taxes.

Current taxation may be required by any of several anti-deferral rules of the U.S. tax law. Special information reporting requirements must also be met by submitting Form 5471, *Information return of U.S. Persons With Respect to Certain Foreign Corporations*. Stockholders who fail to submit the required Form 5471 may be subject to a failure-to-file penalty as well as required to pay the taxes, penalties, and interest on the income required to be reported without the regard to foreign tax credits.

U.S. tax rules for dealing with these complex anti-deferral regimes are beyond the scope of this book.

CHAPTER 6
Income Tax Treaty Benefits

The United States currently has income tax treaties with over 60 countries. U.S. taxpayers who are tax Residents in a country that has an income tax treaty with the United States may be exempt from tax under the provisions of the treaty. Income tax treaties apply to foreign nationals who are tax Residents in the treaty country. Treaties include rules grouped in "articles" by topic or type of income.

Income tax treaties generally cover federal income taxes but not Social Security and Medicare taxes. An exemption from state income taxes may apply indirectly. For example, if a state defines income with reference to federal adjusted gross income and no adjustment is required to include treaty exempt income for state income tax purposes, then treaty exempt income is also exempt from state income taxes.

All treaties include a Saving Clause that allows the United States to tax its Citizens and Residents as if the treaty had not come into force. Therefore, foreign nationals who become Residents under the 183-day residency formula lose income tax treaty benefits unless an exception to the Saving Clause applies. Most treaties include a Saving Clause exception for treaty exemptions under a Teachers and Researchers Article.

(See Chapter 11, "Resources" for where to find more information about tax treaties.)

6.1 U.S. Source Income

Beneficial owners of income who are Nonresidents of the United States and tax Residents in a country with which the United States has a tax treaty may be subject to a lower treaty rate on U.S. source income such as dividends, interest, rents, and royalties.

To obtain the lower rate on withholding, beneficial owners must submit to withholding agents prior to payment a signed and dated Form W-8BEN, *Certificate of Foreign Status of Beneficial Owner for United States Withholding*, prior to the payment of the income. For exemption from tax under a tax treaty, Parts I and II must be completed and the form must include an SSN or ITIN unless the income is from traded securities. (Refer to Chapter 10, "Individual Taxpayer Identification Numbers" for an explanation of the Form W-7 application procedures.)

6.2 Employment Compensation

If the beneficial owner of the compensation is tax resident in a treaty country, a treaty article may apply to avoid U.S. taxation on the income. For example, Article 15 (Dependent Personal Services) of the treaty with Belgium allows an exemption from tax if all the following conditions are met:

- The recipient is present in the United States for a period or periods aggregating less than 183 days in the taxable year.
- The recipient is an employee of a resident of Belgium.
- The income is not borne by a permanent establishment that the employer has in the United States.

Provisions vary by treaty. For example, some treaties require only that the employer not be a resident of the United States. Many newer treaties have a requirement that the foreign national be present for a period of less than 183 days in a 12-month period that begins or ends in the fiscal (calendar) year.

(a) Pre-Relocation Visits

This treaty exception may apply to avoid U.S. taxation for compensation allocable to U.S. work days while on business trips to the United States prior to the date that the foreign national obtained the H-1B Specialty Worker status. Exemptions under this treaty article do not apply for any period in which a foreign national is a Resident of the United States because the Saving Clause includes no exception.

> **EXAMPLE** Hans, a resident of the Belgium, relocated to the United States as an H-1B Worker on April 1, 2005 and became a Resident of the United States. He had visited the United States for a business visit for five days in February and for six days in March beginning March 2, 2005. His residency start date is March 2, 2005 because the combined days from the two visits exceed ten days. However, Hans is able to establish under the tie-breaker rule of Article 4 of the treaty with Belgium that he was a resident of Belgium and a Nonresident of the United States through March 31. Therefore, his residency start date is April 1, 2005.
>
> Even though he is a Nonresident under the treaty, he is still subject to U.S. income taxes on the allocable salary for his earlier visits because his physical presence in the United States exceeds the Article 15 limit of 183 days in the taxable (calendar) year.

(b) Loss of Benefits

Treaty exceptions for employment income do not apply to remuneration paid to foreign nationals for U.S. workdays if the work is performed for a U.S. employer even if paid by a foreign employer. In that case, the IRS considers that the second condition is not met. In situations in which compensation payments made by a foreign employer for services performed for a U.S. employer are cross-charged to the U.S. employer, the IRS considers that the third condition is not met either. This is consistent with the H-1B petition indicating a U.S. company as the employer.

> **EXAMPLE** Pierre, a resident of Belgium, traveled to the United States on business several times before obtaining his H-1B status on October 1, 2005. His foreign employer charged the costs of his services for the earlier visits to its' affiliated U.S. company, which was the primary beneficiary of the services. Even though Pierre spent fewer than 183 days in the United States in 2005, he is not eligible for an exemption from tax under Article 15 for his remuneration paid for his visits while on travel status because it was charged to the U.S. company.

6.3 Compensation of Teachers and Researchers

About three quarters of the tax treaties provide tax treaty benefits to foreign nationals who enter the United States for the primary purpose of teaching or engaging in research. H-1B Specialty Workers can qualify for benefits under the Teachers and Researchers Article if they otherwise meet the conditions of the article. Whether foreign nationals who change status from F-1 or J-1 student status are eligible for treaty benefits varies with the treaty as explained below.

Foreign nationals who were eligible for treaty benefits under a Teachers and Researchers Article while in J-1 Nonstudent status, and who change to H-1B status, may continue to claim the treaty benefit through the end of the treaty benefit period.

> **EXAMPLE** Jan, a resident of Norway, entered the United States August 1, 2004 as a J-1 Professor with an expiration date of July 31, 2005. On July 15, 2005, Jan changed to H-1B status as a professor with an expiration date of July 14, 2008. Jan can claim the benefit of Article 15 (Teachers) from his date of arrival on August 1, 2004 for two years. Even though his immigration status changed his purpose for being in the United States did not.

The IRS has ruled that there is no language in a treaty that requires as a prerequisite for treaty benefits that foreign nationals must have taught in the treaty country prior to teaching in the United States. (See for example Rev. Rul. 69-46, *1969-1 C.B. 235* and Rev. Rul. 70-382, *1970-2 C.B. 331*.)

The IRS has also ruled that the entire remuneration paid to professors or teachers is exempt under a treaty as long as a substantial portion of their time is devoted to teaching, lecturing, and instructing even though they spend a portion of their time devoted to other duties. (See Rev. Rul. 55-211, *1955-1 C.B. 676*.) Under this ruling, researchers who are from a treaty country whose treaty language does not specifically include researchers, (for example, the treaty with Greece) cannot claim treaty benefits for incidental teaching.

(a) Institution Where Teaching or Research Takes Place

The Teachers and Researchers Articles of all treaties provide benefits to those who are teaching or engaged in research (if applicable under the treaty) at a school, college, university or other accredited educational institution. Some treaties substitute the term organization for institution. Some treaties refer to "recognized educational institutions." For purposes of the United States, "recognized" means accredited. Some treaties include other types of institutions as well.

Educational Institution

The term "educational institution" is not defined in the treaties. The Treasury Explanation of Article 20 of the U.S. Model Treaty states that an educational institution is an institution that typically maintains a regular faculty and has a regular body of students in attendance at the place where the educational activities are carried on.

The Treasury Explanation is consistent with the definition of an educational institution in Code Section 170(b)(1)(A)(ii). This Code section defines an "educational institution" as a school maintaining a regular faculty and established curriculum, and having an organized body of students in attendance. This definition includes primary and secondary schools, colleges, universities, normal schools, technical schools, mechanical schools, and similar institutions, but does not include non-educational institutions, on-the-job training, correspondence schools, night schools, and so forth. (Rev. Rul. 81-79, *1981-1 C.B. 605*) To qualify as an educational institution, the primary purpose of the institution, or division thereof, must be educating students. (Rev. Rul. 68-604, *1968-2 C.B. 63*) The branch of a foreign university is an educational institution for treaty purposes if it is an accredited educational institution of the United States. (Rev. Rul. 73-606, *1973-2 C.B. 434*)

Research Institutions

Some Teachers and Researchers Articles include other types of institutions such as research institutions, scientific research institutions, medical facilities primarily funded from government resources, and public research institutions or other institutions engaged in research for the public benefit. The terms "research institution," "scientific research institution," and "public research institution" are intended to cover such institutions as the National Institutes for Health. These additions to the treaty articles are important for such institutions such as NIH, which the IRS has ruled is not an educational institution for purposes of the treaties because NIH lacks a regular faculty, an established curriculum, and an organized body of students and its primary purpose is not to educate students. (Rev. Rul. 75-10, *1975-1 C.B. 389*)

Some of the treaties use the term "recognized research institution." The Treasury Explanation of Article 20 of the treaty with France notes that, "A 'recognized research institution' includes such research facilities as the National Institutes of Health and the Centers for Disease Control."

University Medical Schools and Associated Hospitals

Whether research engaged in at a university hospital associated with a medical school qualifies as research engaged in at an educational institution for purposes of the treaties depends on all the facts and circumstances. The IRS has ruled that a university hospital that had many administrative and functional ties to the university, but was a separate corporation controlled by its own board of trustees, and which maintained no regular faculty and curriculum and had no organized body of students, was not an educational institution. (Rev. Rul. 77-175, *1977-1 C.B. 415*)

For a thorough review of IRS published guidance on the definition of the term "educational institution," refer to ILM 200145040 (23 Aug 2001) which the IRS prepared in response to refund claims by hospitals for medical residents under the Student FICA Exception of section 3121(b)(10). In this memorandum, the IRS stated that a hospital was not a "school, college, or university" for purposes of the Student FICA Exception because the primary purpose of the hospital is patient care. In April 2005, the IRS issued final regulations under section 3121(b)(10) limiting the definition of "school, college, or university" for purposes of the Student FICA Exception to institutions which have as their primary purpose educating students. This regulation does not appear to change the earlier IRS rulings that allow treaty benefits in situations in which a division of an institution has educating students as its primary purpose.

Even though the institution may not be an educational institution, foreign nationals may nevertheless be entitled to a treaty benefit if their common law employer is an educational institution. For example, the IRS determined that a research fellow who was appointed to the faculty of an accredited university's medical school and who conducted basic research in the public's interest under the school's direction and control in a laboratory located in a hospital associated with the school was exempt from tax. Based on the facts and circumstances in the ruling, the hospital did not exercise control over the laboratory research even though the laboratory was located in the university hospital and the foreign national's compensation was paid by the university hospital. The foreign national was performing research under the supervision and control of the university medical school, an accredited educational institution and was, therefore, the common law employee of the educational institution. (Rev. Rul. 81-79, *1981-1 C.B. 605*) For a thorough analysis of employment relationships of medical residents and how the IRS determines the common law employer, refer to ILM200029030.

(b) Article Limitations

In order for professors, teachers and researchers to qualify for exemption from tax under a Teachers and Researchers Article, they must meet the qualifying conditions of the specific tax treaty article. Foreign nationals engaged in research have some additional considerations described in Section 6.3 below.

Benefit Period

Most Teachers and Researchers Articles exempt all remuneration from personal services for teaching or research from tax for a period not exceeding two years. The treaty with Greece provides a three-year benefit period. The IRS has ruled that the period of exemption begins on the date foreign nationals first visit the United States for the purpose of teaching or engaging in research. (Rev. Rul. 89-5, *1989-1 C.B. 353*)

> **EXAMPLE** Paola, a resident of Italy, entered the United States on August 1, 2005 as a teacher in H-1B status with an expiration date of July 31, 2008. Article 20 (Professors and Teachers) of the treaty with Italy provides no starting date for the two-year benefit. Paola is exempt from tax from August 1, 2005, her date of arrival for the purpose of teaching, through July 31, 2007.

The period of exemption is not affected by earlier visits to the United States for other purposes, such as personal vacations, during which no treaty benefits were claimed.

Under the two oldest treaties still in effect, the treaty with Pakistan and the treaty with Greece, the exemption is lost if foreign nationals become Residents of the United States. These treaties have no Saving Clause exceptions. The exemption remains applicable to income earned during the period before they became Residents for tax purposes.

> **EXAMPLE** Stella, a resident of Greece, entered the United States on August 1, 2005 as a teacher in H-1B status with an expiration date of July 31, 2008. Stella can claim the benefit of Article XII [Teachers] for 2005 because she is a Nonresident. She cannot claim the benefit of Article XII for subsequent years when she is a Resident because Article XIV saves the right of the United States to tax its Residents with no exceptions.

Article 19 [Teachers and Researchers] of the treaty with China contains a unique benefit period. Residents of China are exempt from tax on the remuneration for such teaching or research for a period "not exceeding three years in the aggregate." The majority of foreign nationals claiming the benefits of this article do so over a three-year period beginning with the date of arrival in the United States.

> **EXAMPLE** Won, a resident of China, entered the United States on August 1, 2005 as a teacher in H-1B status with an expiration date of July 31, 2008. Won can claim the benefit of Article 19 [Teachers and Researchers] through the end of the three-year benefit period. He is a Nonresident for 2005 and a Resident for 2006 through 2008. Article 2 of the Protocol of the treaty with China, saves the right of the United States to tax its Residents except for specified articles of the treaty which includes Article 19.

However, residents of China may claim the three-year benefit during periods that can be spread over a number of years as long as they meet the other conditions of the treaty article for each visit. Such an interpretation is permissible because:

- "In the aggregate," used in other treaty articles such as Income from Employment Article and Income from Self-employment Articles means "the whole sum of the amount."
- The Treasury Explanation of Article 19 makes it clear that the three years are not consecutive years from the date of arrival.
- IRS Rev. Rul. 89-5, which applied the date-of-arrival rule to the Teachers and Researchers Articles, specifically left out Article 19 of the treaty with China.

> **EXAMPLE** Chou, a resident of China, enters the United States periodically for the purpose of engaging in research at a University in California. He remains domiciled in China, and subject to taxes there as a resident. He is eligible to claim a benefit under Article 19 [Teachers and Researchers] until the three-years in the aggregate (1095 days) is used up. He should detail the treaty benefits claimed for prior visits each time he submits his U.S. tax return.

Prospective Loss of Benefits

A number of articles provide treaty benefits to teachers and researchers who are invited to come to the United States for a period "not expected to exceed two years." If the initial period for the visit exceeds two years, they are not eligible for the benefit. If their initial visit is for less than two years but is later extended to beyond two years, the exemption is not lost. It applies to their income from personal services for teaching or research received before the expiration of the two-year period.

> **EXAMPLE 1** Sven, a resident of the Norway, entered the United States on August 1, 2003 in H-1B status as a teacher with an expiration date of July 31, 2006. Sven is not eligible to claim the benefit of Article 15 (Teachers) because the article limits benefits to teachers whose stay in the United States is "not expected to exceed two years." His stay is expected to last for three years based on his immigration documents.
>
> **EXAMPLE 2** Jan, a resident of Norway, entered the United States August 1, 2004 as a J-1 Professor with an expiration date of July 31, 2005. On July 15, 2005, Jan changed to H-1B status as a professor with an expiration date of July 14, 2008. Jan can claim the benefit of Article 15 (Teachers) from his date of arrival on August 1, 2004 for two years. His initial immigration period was not expected to exceed two years. The fact that he later changed status with a new expiration date which caused his stay to exceed two years does not cause him to lose the benefit of Article 15.

Retroactive Loss of Benefits

The Teachers and Researchers Articles of treaties with six countries — Germany, India, Luxembourg, the Netherlands, Thailand, and the U.K. — include a retroactive loss of benefits provision. Under this provision, if a foreign national's physical presence in the United States exceeds the two-year benefit period, the benefit is lost retroactively to the first dollar. This retroactive reflects the U.S. Government policy that such benefits should be limited to temporary visits for professors, teachers, and researchers who will return to the treaty country and not stay on for indefinite employment in the United States.

> **EXAMPLE** Magda, a resident of the Germany, entered the United States on August 1, 2003 as a teacher and claimed a benefit under Article 20(1) (Visiting Professors and Teachers) through July 31, 2005. Magda remained in the United States to teach a summer course until September 15, 2005. She lost the treaty benefit retroactively because she failed to meet the condition of Article 18 of the Protocol to the treaty with Germany which allows the United States to tax her compensation retroactive to the beginning of the benefit period because she failed to leave timely.

Under some but not all of these treaties, if the competent authorities agree in a particular case, the exemption may apply for the two years even if their stay exceeds two years. This exception requires that foreign nationals first pay the tax and deal with procedures, described in Rev. Proc. 96-13, *1996-1 C.B. 616*, which involves both Governments in the process. The competent authorities agree to such an extension only in cases where the departure after the end of the two-year period is caused by unforeseen circumstances outside of the control of both the foreign national and the institution.

One time Use

Some newer treaties restrict the number of times that foreign nationals can claim exemption under the Teachers and Researchers Article to a one-time benefit. Thus, for example, foreign nationals who spend one or two years teaching in the United States and claim the treaty benefit, then leave for a year, and return to teach or engage in research again, may not claim the exemption during the second visit.

> **EXAMPLE 1** Catherine, a resident of France, entered the United States on August 1, 2003 as a teacher for a one-year period that ended on July 31, 2004. She claimed a treaty benefit under Article 20 of the treaty with France which has a one-time use limit. Catherine entered the United States as a teacher again on August 1, 2005. She may not claim a treaty benefit again even though she did not use up the two-year benefit during her first visit.

> **EXAMPLE 2** Vanessa, a resident of France, entered the United States on August 1, 2004 as a teacher for a six-month period that ended on January 31, 2005. She claimed a treaty benefit under Article 20 of the treaty that has a one-time use limit. Vanessa entered the United States as a teacher again on August 1, 2005. She may claim the treaty benefit from August 1, 2005 through July 31, 2006 because this is within the two-year benefit period that began with her first entry as a teacher on August 1, 2004.

Although not specifically stated in the treaty text, the Treasury Explanation of the treaty with China makes it clear that the three-year in the aggregate benefit may only be used one time as well.

(c) Successive Treaty Article Claims

Foreign nationals who meet the qualifications of a Teachers and Researchers Article may again claim its benefits if they first reestablish tax residence in the treaty country. In such cases, they may claim these benefits on a subsequent occasion if they establish physical presence and residency in the treaty country and are absent from the United States for at least one year (365 days). (Rev. Rul. 77-242, *1977-2C.B. 489*)The IRS follows the same rule in allowing consecutive benefits for Students and Trainees Articles followed by benefits from Teachers and Researchers Articles. Foreign nationals are not allowed by the IRS to claim consecutive treaty benefits unless the treaty includes specific provisions for consecutive exemptions.

EXAMPLE Wolfgang, a resident of the Germany, entered the United States on August 1, 2001 as a teacher and claimed a benefit under Article 20(1) (Visiting Professors and Teachers) through July 1, 2003. Wolfgang entered the United States again on August 15, 2005. He can claim the benefits of Article 20(1) because he reestablished residency in Germany and was absent from the United States for a year (365 days).

(d) Combined Benefit Periods

A number of treaties limit the combined benefits of the Students and Trainees and Teachers and Researchers Articles to a total combined period of no more than five years. Most treaties specify taxable years, but some specify only (elapsed) years. The combination of consecutive exemptions may not extend beyond the specified five-year period from the date the foreign nationals arrived for purposes of the first Students and Trainees Article. Treaties with such combined benefit periods allow consecutive article claims unless the treaty indicates otherwise. Under this provision, the exemption applies to income received by foreign nationals before the expiration of such combined period.

EXAMPLE Hans, a resident of Belgium, entered the United States as a student on August 1, 2001. He claimed a treaty benefit while a student. Hans changed status to a research scholar on July 1, 2005. The combined benefit period of Article 21(4) limits his benefit period to five taxable years from August 1, 2001. His benefit period ends December 31, 2005. The treaty with Belgium has no back-to-back limitation to prevent his benefit claim.

(e) Back-to-back Limitations

A number of treaties make it clear that the benefits provided by the Teachers and Researchers Articles are not available to foreign nationals if, during the immediately preceding period, they enjoyed the benefits of the Students and Trainees Article. Treasury Explanations of this limitation make it clear that, in order to claim Teachers and Researchers Article benefits after having claimed Students and Trainees Article benefits, foreign nationals must reestablish physical presence and residency in the treaty country and be physically absent from the United States for a period of at least one year (365 days).

EXAMPLE 1 Josef, a resident of Israel, entered the United States as a student on August 1, 2001. He claimed no treaty benefits while a student. Josef changed status to a research scholar on July 1, 2005. The combined benefit period of Article 24(4) limits his benefit period to five taxable years from August 1, 2001. His Article 23 (Teachers) benefit period ends December 31, 2005. The back-to-back limitation does not prevent his claim under Article 23 (Teachers) since he claimed no benefit under Article 24 (Students and Trainees).

EXAMPLE 2 Ari, a resident of Israel, entered the United States as a student on August 1, 1999. He claimed a treaty benefit while a student. He returned to Israel and reestablished residency and physical presence on June 15, 2003. Ari entered the United States again as a research scholar on July 1, 2004. The combined benefit period of Article 24(4) does not apply. His Article 23 (Teachers) two-year benefit period ends June 30, 2006. The back-to-back limitation of Article 24(4) does not prevent his Article 23 (Teachers) claim because he reestablished residency in Israel and was absent from the United States for one year (365 days).

6.4 Special Considerations for Research Scholars

Foreign nationals who enter the United States for the primary purpose of engaging in research may be entitled to claim an exemption from tax under a Teachers and Researchers Article of a tax treaty. Researchers have a number of additional conditions to meet in order to claim such a benefit.

(a) Compensation for Services vs. Scholarship or Fellowship

Foreign nationals who are teaching are performing services. Whether researchers are being compensated for services or being provided a fellowship grant for engaging in research without a requirement to provide services is not always as clear when the foreign national is engaged in research while in J-1 Nonstudent status. However, for H-1B Workers, payments have been characterized to the immigration service as wages under the prevailing wage requirement of an H-1B petition and supporting documentation. Remuneration paid to an H-1B Worker is considered wages for income tax purposes as well as for immigration purposes, because immigration law requires there to be an employer-employee relationship between the sponsor and the foreign national being sponsored.

(b) Public Benefit Requirement

Teacher/Researcher Articles of all treaties, except for the treaty with China, specify that for the treaty exemption to apply to income from research, the research must be undertaken in the public interest and not primarily for the private benefit of a specific person or persons. For example, research projects which are undertaken to discover or perfect product processes, designs, etc., which are expected to be commercially exploited by the researcher or his present (or former) employer do not qualify under this limitation. Likewise, the exemption does not apply to grants from tax-exempt research organizations to search for the cure for a disease if the results of the research become the property of a for-profit company. The exemption does apply, however, if the tax-exempt organization licenses the results of the research to a for-profit enterprise in consideration of an arm's-length royalty consistent with its tax-exempt status.

The treaty with the Former USSR, which covers the Newly Independent States (NIS) that have not yet negotiated their own treaty with the United States, includes a provision that income from research conducted pursuant to an intergovernmental agreement on cooperation would still be exempt, regardless of the beneficiary of the research.

CHAPTER 7
State Income Taxes

Forty-one states and the District of Columbia impose income taxes on the income of foreign nationals. The rules for determining residency for state income tax purposes vary by state and may be different from the federal rules described in Chapter 2, "U.S. Tax Residency Rules."

Foreign nationals' state tax status may be different from their federal tax status. For example, depending on the circumstances, a foreign national could be:

- A nonresident for state income tax purposes and a Resident for federal income tax purposes
- A resident for state income tax purposes and a Nonresident for federal income tax purposes
- A nonresident for state income tax purposes and a Nonresident for federal income tax purposes
- A resident for state income tax purposes and a Resident for federal income tax purposes

Some states tie their tax residency rules to the federal status or to foreign nationals' U.S. immigration status. For example, in Wisconsin:

- Foreign nationals who are Nonresidents for federal purposes for the full year are treated as nonresidents for Wisconsin income tax purposes.
- Foreign nationals who are Residents for federal purposes for all or part of the year may be either residents or nonresidents for Wisconsin purposes.
- Nonimmigrants such as H-1B Workers are nonresidents.
- Nonimmigrants who become U.S. Lawful Permanent Residents (LPRs) become residents of Wisconsin for tax purpose.

States typically impose income taxes on individuals domiciled in the state. Many states also impose income taxes on individuals who are physically present in the state for a specified number of days. State tax authorities generally post their tax forms and helpful publications describing their state's residency rules on their websites, which can be found through www.taxadmin.org.

7.1 Domicile

Most states impose income taxes on individuals who are domiciled in the state. Domicile is a legal concept that means an individual has a residence in the state accompanied by proof that the individual intends to stay there indefinitely. For example, Massachusetts has a domicile rule. Nonimmigrants such as H-1B Specialty Workers who reside in Massachusetts for a temporary period after which time they will return to their home country are not considered domiciled in Massachusetts unless the facts indicate otherwise. However, foreign nationals residing temporarily in Massachusetts who become U.S. Lawful Permanent Residents (LPR) become domiciled in Massachusetts if that is where they reside. By definition, an LPR intends to reside permanently in the United States.

7.2 Residence

Many states also impose income tax on individuals who are residents in the state for a specific period of time. For example, Massachusetts imposes income taxes on the worldwide income of an individual who maintains a permanent place of abode in Massachusetts, and who spends more than 183 days in Massachusetts in the calendar year. Days include partial days in Massachusetts. This physical presence rule includes an exception for individuals who are on an assignment anticipated to last a year or less who otherwise meet the residency test. Nonimmigrants such as H-1B Workers who relocate to Massachusetts and who are not physically present in the state for 183 days are Nonresidents. This is frequently the case for the individual's first year of presence in the state.

7.3 State Tax Rules

The rules for determining income, deductions and the tax rates vary by state. For information on a particular state's income tax rules and forms visit the state tax authority's website. Visit www.taxadmin.org for links to the applicable website.

7.4 Income Tax Treaty Exemptions

Income tax treaties by the terms of the Taxes Covered Article of each treaty apply to federal income taxes. State income taxes are not mentioned by the treaties. However, an income tax treaty exemption may apply to state income taxes indirectly. Many states define income based on federal income (federal gross income, federal adjusted gross income, or federal taxable income). In these situations, if the income is exempt from federal income tax under a treaty, the income is also exempt from state income taxes. For example, Massachusetts defines income with reference to federal gross income with some adjustments. Since Massachusetts does not require that treaty exempt income be added back into income for state income tax purposes, the treaty exempt income is exempt from Massachusetts income taxes as well. Some states, Connecticut for example, require that treaty-exempt income be taken into account for state tax purposes.

Income exempt by treaty from federal income tax is not exempt from state income tax in the following states:

Alabama	Hawaii	Maryland	New Jersey
Arkansas	Kansas	Mississippi	North Dakota
California	Kentucky	Montana	Pennsylvania
Connecticut			

Note: Montana and North Dakota may allow the treaty exemption on a tax return but do not allow an exemption from withholding.

CHAPTER 8
Withholding and Reporting

Wages include all amounts paid by employers to or on behalf of employees, including the fair market value of fringe benefits unless an exception applies to exclude the fringe benefits from tax. Fringe benefits include benefits provided in kind by employers, such as housing, and reimbursements made to third parties by employers on the behalf of employees, such as for shipping. Wages paid to or on behalf of L-1 Transferees by foreign employers for services performed for U.S. employers are subject to U.S. wage withholding by the U.S. employer and wage reporting on Form W-2.

These obligations are explained in IRS Rev. Rul. 92-106, *1992-2 C.B. 258*.

8.1 Benefits in Kind

The extent to which reimbursements and allowances such as for travel and lodging are includable in U.S. gross income depends upon the length of the assignment and the method of payment. Certain employee business expenses, such as travel, food, and lodging are deductible by employees who are temporarily away from their tax homes.

(a) Temporarily-Away-From-Home vs. Relocation

Expenses that can be deducted as business expenses by employees can be excluded from income as working condition fringe benefits if they meet the IRS' accountable plan rules. To meet the accountable plan rules, employees must:

- Establish the business purpose for the payment
- Substantiate the expenses claimed to the employer
- Reimburse the employer in a reasonable time any amounts that are over and above the substantiated business expenses

If employees do not meet the temporarily-away-from-home criteria, or travel, food, and lodging are not reimbursed through an accountable plan, the reimbursements and in-kind benefits are subject to wage withholding and Form W-2 income reporting.

Employees who have changed their tax homes to the new location may be entitled to claim qualified moving expense deductions for some of the expenses. As described below, employers who pay or reimburses such qualified moving expenses may exclude these expenses from employees' gross wages.

(b) Tax Home

Employees' tax homes are their main place of business or employment. If employees have no main place of business because of the nature of their business, their tax home is their principal place of abode in a real and substantial sense. In controversies with the IRS on the location of employees' tax homes, courts have place a significant amount of weight on whether or not the employees had duplicate living expenses.

IRS issued Rev. Rul. 93-86, *1993-2 C.B. 71*, to assist employers and taxpayers in determining when tax homes change to the new work location. Under this revenue ruling:

- Employees on temporary work assignments anticipated to last one year or less are not considered to have changed their tax homes to the United States.

- Employees on temporary work assignments anticipated to last a year or less, but whose work assignment is extended beyond one year by their employer, are considered to have changed their tax homes to the United States from the date on which their assignment is extended.

- Employees on work assignments anticipated to last more than one year are considered to have changed their tax homes to the United States from the outset of their assignments.

Employees whose tax homes have changed to the new work location in the United States are not eligible for deductions for travel, food, and lodging at the work location. Therefore, to the extent that these expenses are paid or reimbursed by employers, they are subject to wage withholding and Form W-2 wage reporting.

Employees who have been on a temporary work assignment of a year or less, and who return to their tax home, may have a subsequent temporary work assignment covered by these rules as long as there is sufficient time between the assignments to "restart the clock." The IRS has not issued any revenue rulings on the length of time between assignments needed to restart the clock. However, IRS legal memoranda state that a short break of two to three weeks will not restart the clock but a continuous break of seven months during which the employee is absent from the work location is a significant break in service and will restart the clock.

(c) Temporarily Away-From-Home Expenses

Payments and reimbursements that qualify as temporarily-away-from-home expenses are deductible by the employee as miscellaneous itemized deductions to the extent that the combined expenses exceed two percent of adjusted gross income. Reimbursed expenses can include reimbursements for airfare, local transportation such as taxis, food, lodging, laundry and tips. They do not include personal expenses such as payments made to or on behalf of employees' accompanying family members.

Temporarily-away-from-home expense reimbursements made by employers meeting the accountable plan rules are excludable from wage withholding and are not includable in the employee's Form w-2 gross wages. (Refer to IRS Publication 463, *Travel, Entertainment, Gift and Car Expenses*, for more information about these rules.)

(d) Per Diems

Special rules related to the payment of per diems in lieu of reimbursed expenses apply to limit the inclusion of per diems in income of employees who meet the temporarily-away-from-home criteria. Under these rules, the excludable per diem amounts are limited to the meals and incidentals (M&I) amounts when the cost of housing is paid directly by employers or reimbursed based on actual expenses. Otherwise, per diem amounts are limited to combined M&I and lodging amounts for employees. The per diem amounts exceeding the limitations are subject to wage withholding and Form W-2 wage reporting. The substantiation rules for per diem amounts are explained in detail in Rev. Proc. 2005-67, *2005-42 I.R.B. 1,* which provides the maximum standard per diem amounts. This Revenue Procedure is updated periodically. Report the substantiated amounts in Box 12 of Form W-2 using code L.

The IRS provides per diem amounts by locality in the continental United States (called CONUS). The U.S. State Department provides per diems for non-foreign localities outside the United States (OCONUS) including Alaska, Hawaii, Puerto Rico, and U.S. possessions as well as for foreign locations. Per diem amounts by location are available in IRS Publication 1542, *Per Diem Rates, (for Travel within the Continental United States)*, and on www.policyworks.gov.

(e) Company-Provided Automobiles

When employers provide their employees with automobiles for both business and personal use, only the value of the business use is excludable as a working condition fringe benefit.

The working condition fringe benefit exclusion is determined with reference to the portion of the value of an automobile based on its business use. This proportionate value may be determined as a percentage of business use or based on business miles driven. The IRS allows the business use to be determined on a sampling basis, i.e. one week per month or three months per year, when the sample is representative of actual use. However, when employers treat a portion of the value as personal without adequate supporting records, the total value is includable in gross wages.

Value of Owned Automobiles

Special valuation rules apply to determine the value of company-provided automobiles for purposes of determining the amount includable in gross wages. Under these special rules, the Annual Lease Value (ALV) for determining the income inclusion for the use of a provided automobile owned by employers is about $500 plus 25 percent of the automobile's fair market value as of the first year that the rule is used.

Value of Leased Automobiles

When employers lease automobiles provided to their employees, the fair market value can be determined under one of three methods: 1) the retail value of the automobile from a recognized valuation guide, 2) the manufacturers' suggested retail price, including sales tax, title and other direct expenses of purchase, less a discount of eight percent, or 3) the manufacturers' invoice price plus four percent. Automobiles valued at more than $17,500 must include an additional amount in the valuation provided by IRS tables. Refer to Rev. Proc. 2004-20, *2004-13 I.R.B. 642* for tables of applicable additional amounts based on vehicle type.

Reportable Value

The fair market value (FMV) includable in the employee's wages is prorated between personal use and commuting use by multiplying the value of the automobile as determined above by a fraction determined by dividing the total personal and commuting mileage by the total mileage. For an assignment of a year or less, commuting to work at the assignment location is considered business and not personal use for purposes of this formula. If the personal and commuting mileage is unknown, the full value is reportable. Company-paid expenses related to the provided automobile such as insurance are also reportable and subject to proration under these rules.

Cents per Mile Alternative

Employers providing less-expensive automobiles which are used at least 50 percent in the employer's business or driven at least 10,000 miles in the year by the employee, may use a standard mileage rate to value personal miles. The standard mileage rate is 44.5 cents for 2006. The standard rate, which includes the cost of gasoline, can be used for employees driving more than one automobile.

(f) Moving Expenses

Employees who change their tax homes to the United States may be able to claim deductions for certain moving expenses they pay and for certain expenses paid by their employers to the extent that payments made by their employers have not been excluded from Form W-2 gross wages. In order for moving expenses to be deductible, employees must be employed at the new location full time for at least 39 weeks in the 12-month period following the move. In addition, the distance between an employee's new work location and old residence must be at least 50 miles further than between the employee's prior work location and his old residence.

Under U.S. tax rules, moving expenses relate to the compensation to be earned at the new location. This rule is referred to as the "forward attribution rule." If the future compensation is not subject to U.S. tax, as would be the case for relocations abroad by foreign nationals, the moving expenses are not deductible with one exception. If an employer agrees to reimburse the costs of the relocation home in writing at the outset of the assignment, the moving expenses are considered attributable to the U.S. assignment and, therefore, are deductible. Although there is no IRS ruling on the matter, the fact that the U.S. employer is required under the immigration laws to reimburse the costs of the relocation home of H-1B Specialty Workers should be sufficient to satisfy the written requirement rule. However, this immigration rule only applies to the transportation costs for the employee, not for accompanying family members.

Only expenses for travel, the transportation of household goods to the new location, and storage expenses incurred in transit are deductible. If paid directly by employers or reimbursed through expense vouchers, these expenses are not includable in Form W-2 gross wages. Expenses that are reimbursed to employees are reportable in Box 12 of the Form W-2 with Code P. Amounts paid directly to third parties are not reportable. All other moving expenses, such as house hunting and interim living reimbursements, are subject to wage withholding and are reportable in Form W-2 gross wages. Lump sum payments made to employees are treated as wages subject to withholding and reporting.

(g) Pension Plan Contributions

Only pension contributions to U.S. qualified plans are excludable from gross wages. Frequently, employees and their foreign employers continue to make contributions to foreign plans on behalf of employees working in the United States. Contributions made to foreign plans by employees working in the United States do not reduce gross wages for U.S. tax purposes. Contributions made by foreign employers are considered wages subject to wage withholding and reporting in Form W-2 gross wages unless a tax treaty exception applies. Only a few income tax treaties include provisions relating to the U.S. tax treatment of such contributions.

Foreign national employees working in the United States for U.S. employers are eligible to be included in U.S. qualified plans. The taxation of distributions from these plans when employees relocate home depends on 1) the employee's country of tax residency at the time of distribution, 2) whether that country has an income tax treaty with the United States, and 3) the terms of an applicable income tax treaty relating to such distributions, if any.

(h) Tax Return Preparation Fees

Many companies that transfer employees to and from the United States provide and pay for the services of a designated accounting or tax firm to prepare the employee's U.S. and foreign tax returns. The services are typically provided as part of companies' tax reimbursement or equalization program. Companies retain the services of an experienced accounting or tax firm 1) to advise the company and their employee on tax obligations, 2) to recommend tax saving opportunities, 3) to assure that tax returns and necessary extensions are prepared correctly and timely, and 4) to prepare the tax reimbursement or equalization computations.

The IRS views the value of employer-provided tax preparation services to be a taxable fringe benefit includable in employees' wages because the services primarily benefit the employee. An employer that provides tax preparation services for its transferred employees needs to request invoices that separately state the tax preparation services provided for each employee in order to determine the value of the includable income. Other services that benefit the employer such as tax reimbursement or equalization computations should be separately stated to avoid issues on income inclusion.

(i) Immigration Fees

Immigration processing fees and attorney fees for obtaining nonimmigrant status authorizing employment, such as H-1B Specialty Worker status, are ordinary and necessary expenses of the business because the petition is the responsibility of the employer, not the employee. Such fees are not includable in the employee's income.

Sponsoring employers need to use caution when having H-1B Workers pay their own immigration fees. The U.S. Department of Labor (DOL) agrees that the H-1B Worker may pay immigration fees other than the special H-1B fee. However, when the H-1B Worker pays the fees (including any related legal fees), the DOL deducts them from the worker's actual wage for prevailing wage purposes. If the H-1B's net wage falls below the prevailing wage as a result, the sponsoring employer has committed an actionable wage violation. The payment of these fees by the H-1B worker is not a problem as long as the net wage exceeds the prevailing wage.

Whether other immigration processing fees and attorney fees are excludable from income depends on whether, under the facts, the expenses are a deductible business expense of the employee. If so, then the expenses would be excludable from income as a working condition fringe benefit. If not, the expenses are includable as wages. For example, fees in support of U.S. lawful permanent residency status for employees nearing end of the maximum time period of their nonimmigrant status are deductible business expenses if the employer requires the services of the employee to continue. Fees related to family members are personal and are not deductible.

8.2 Special Withholding Rules for Nonresidents

The withholding rules for payments to foreign nationals who are Residents follow the same rules as for U.S. Citizens. The withholding rules for Nonresidents are different from the withholding rules for U.S. Citizens and Residents because they mirror the tax return rules for Nonresidents. Special rules apply to limit exemptions and deductions that Nonresidents can use for tax return purposes. In addition, married Nonresidents cannot submit joint tax returns with a Nonresident spouse. The withholding rules for compensation paid to Nonresidents include special rules to reflect these limitations.

- **Nonresidents can only use single status.** This rule applies because married Nonresidents cannot submit a tax return using married filing jointly rates. Since Nonresidents must use the higher married filing separately rates for tax return filing purposes, the IRS requires that they use the higher single rates for withholding. (There is no wage withholding table for married filing separately status.)
- **Nonresidents can only claim one personal exemption unless an exception applies.** Exceptions are available for residents of Canada and Mexico; residents of South Korea under certain circumstances; business apprentices students from India and nationals of American Samoa and the Northern Mariana Islands.
- **Nonresidents must indicate "Nonresident Alien" or "NRA" on the line 6 of Form W-4.** Nonresident employees must be identified because withholding on wages of Nonresident employees is different from that of U.S. Citizens and Residents as noted above. Also the withholding on wages of Nonresident employees must be calculated using a special adjustment because the standard deduction is built into the wage tables. Nonresidents cannot claim the standard deduction (with an exception of certain business apprentices and students from India.)

See IRS Notice 2005-76, *2005-46 I.R.B.*, for more information about these procedures.

(a) Residency Change Year

Foreign nationals who become Residents under the 183-day residency formula in the calendar year are treated as Residents retroactively to their first day of U.S. presence in the year. This date is called the "residency start date". However, foreign nationals who remain residents of a treaty country, and who are U.S. Nonresidents under the treaty tie-breaker rule, may use a Form 8833 or similar statement to claim nonresidency status for withholding and tax return purposes.

This look-back rule for determining the residency start date was designed for tax return purposes, but wage withholding is prospective. The IRS has published no guidance to date on when foreign nationals are to be treated as Residents for wage withholding tax purposes in the calendar year in which they become Residents. Because of the lack of guidance, employers apply the rules inconsistently some using the residency start date and some using the date that the 183-day residency formula is satisfied (called the "residency change date").

The IRS' current audit position is to treat foreign nationals as Residents from the residency start date. Employers who use this rule may treat foreign nationals as Nonresidents when they know that they will remain Nonresidents because of plans to repatriate before they become Residents.

(b) Full-year Residency Elections

Nonresidents who will become Residents by calendar year end, or who are married to U.S. Citizens or Residents, can elect to be treated as Residents for the full calendar year. Under these rules (explained in more detail in Chapter 3, "Residency Start and Termination Dates") Nonresidents can elect to be treated as Residents for wage withholding purposes as well as for tax return purposes. To make this election, Nonresidents must submit a statement to their employer, dated and signed under the penalties of perjury, that they will meet the criteria for, and will submit, a U.S. federal tax return as Residents for the calendar year.

8.3 Treaty Exempt Compensation

In order to claim exemption from income tax withholding under an income tax treaty provision, foreign nationals must submit a special form to their employer prior to the payment for exemption from withholding under an income tax treaty. (Refer to Chapter 6, "Income Tax Treaty Benefits" for an explanation of the income tax treaty exemptions that may apply to payments to H-1B Specialty Workers.) The type of form depends on whether they are claiming treaty benefits as Nonresidents or Residents. Foreign nationals becoming Residents during the calendar year are treated as Residents retroactive to their first countable day of presence in the United States in the calendar year. In such cases, the IRS audit position is that they be treated as Residents from that date for withholding purposes.

(a) Form 8233 for Nonresident Treaty Claims

Nonresidents claiming exemption from tax on compensation for services under an income tax treaty must submit completed Form 8233, *Exemption from Withholding on Compensation*, accompanied by a certifying statement for under the treaty article that the treaty benefit is being claimed. The IRS has published certifying statements in revenue procedures for treaties effective through 1993. Refer to IRS Publication 901, *U.S. Tax Treaties*, for certification statements. For later treaties for which the IRS has provided no certification, the payer may accept a certification that agrees with the conditions of the Teachers and Researchers Article under which treaty benefits are being claimed.

Employers must submit the form to the IRS for approval within five days of receipt. Employers may begin exempting compensation from withholding from the outset. However, if the IRS later determines that an exemption is not allowable, the employer must collect the underwithheld taxes to avoid liability for the underwithheld taxes, penalties and interest. Foreign nationals claiming treaty exemptions on compensation must submit a new Form 8233 for each calendar year in which the treaty exemption is being claimed.

The processing of Forms 8233 has been transferred to the Philadelphia Submission Processing Center. Employers must mail forms to the following address:

> Internal Revenue Service
> International Returns Section
> P.O. Box 920
> Bensalem, PA 19020-8518

Alternatively, employers may fax Form 8233 and its attachments to the following fax numbers in Philadelphia: (215) 516-1506, (215) 516-1507, or (215) 516-3216. A maximum of 15 pages may be faxed at any one time. The IRS prefers that the Forms 8233 be faxed instead of mailed. A Form 8233 that has been faxed to the IRS should **not** be sent by hard copy.

(b) Form W-9 for Residents' Treaty Claims

Residents who qualify for income tax treaty exemption under exceptions to a treaty's Saving Clause must submit a Form W-9 with an attachment that includes the following information:

- Name and U.S. taxpayer identification number
- A statement that the foreign national is a Resident under the substantial presence test
- The tax treaty country and treaty article under which the exemption is claimed, and a description of the article
- A statement that the foreign national is relying on an exception to the saving clause for the exemption

Unlike Form 8233, which must be submitted to the IRS, Form W-9 is for the employer's records only and should not be sent to the IRS. There is no regulatory requirement that the Form W-9 be submitted annually. However, requesting such a submission assures employers that the facts supporting the treaty claim have not changed.

(c) Taxpayer Identification Number Requirement

Employers cannot allow treaty exemptions from withholding if the withholding certificate submitted by the foreign national does not have a taxpayer identification number (TIN). For foreign nationals with work authorization, the appropriate TIN is a Social Security number (SSN). Form 8233 instructions allow an exemption from withholding to be claimed even if an SSN has not yet been received. Employees may attach a copy of Form SS-5 evidencing the application for the SSN. Although not mentioned by the current instructions, the IRS also accepts a copy of or a receipt for an SSN application from the Social Security Administration. If an employer allows a treaty exemption in a situation in which the SSN has been applied, but is not received by the time the employer must submit the Form 1042-S tax return, they will be assessed the underwithheld tax plus penalties and interest by the IRS.

(d) Form 1042 and 1042-S Requirements

Compensation exempt from tax under a tax treaty must be reported on a Form 1042-S, *Foreign Person's U.S. Source Income Subject to Withholding*, rather than on Form W-2. Form W-2 gross federal wages must be reduced by the amount reported on the Form 1042-S. The Form 1042-S Income Code for teaching or engaging in research is 18.

Any employer submitting a Form 1042-S must submit a Form 1042, *Annual Withholding Tax Return for U.S. Source Income of Foreign Persons*, as well. Forms 1042 and 1042-S are due March 15. Paper submissions to the IRS must be accompanied by a Form 1042-T, *Annual Summary and Transmittal of Forms 1042-S*. For more information on submitting these forms, refer to *A Guide to Filing IRS Forms 1042 and 1042-S*.

(e) Coordination with Form W-2 Reporting

Treaty exempt compensation must not be reported on Form W-2. Rather, such income must be reported on Form 1042-S. Many payroll systems producing Form W-2 cannot automatically reduce Form W-2 federal gross wages for compensation reported on Form 1042-S. Employers using such systems must manually reduce Form W-2 federal gross wages by Form 1042-S treaty exempt amount in order to avoid reporting the amount twice.

Treaty exempt compensation reported on Form 1042-S that is exempt from state income taxes as well may also be reported on Form 1042-S. If the state income is not exempt under the treaty, the state wages and withholding must be reported on Form W-2.

If all of wages are exempt under a treaty, the wages are reported on Form 1042-S and the federal gross wages on Form W-2 is blank. If some, but not all, of the wages are exempt under a treaty, the treaty exempt amount is reported on Form 1042-S and the taxable wages and withholding are reported on Form W-2. This typically occurs in the last calendar year in which a teacher's or researcher's treaty benefit ends.

> **EXAMPLE** Pierre, a professor from France, entered the United States to teach on August 15, 2003. His two-year benefit period ends August 14, 2005. He continues teaching beyond the end of his benefit period in 2005. Pierre's treaty exempt compensation is reported on Form 1042-S. His taxable compensation for teaching after August 14, 2005 is reported on Form W-2 in federal gross wages.

Social Security and Medicare wages and taxes are reported on Form W-2 even if all wages are exempt from income tax under a treaty. The treaty exempt income is reported on Form 1042-S. This typically occurs with treaty exempt payments to a teacher or researcher in H-1B status, since the foreign national, with few exceptions, is not exempt from Social Security and Medicare taxes as explained below.

8.4 Social Security and Medicare Taxes

United States law provides compulsory Social Security coverage for services performed in the United States as an employee. The citizenship or country of residence of the employee or employer is not relevant nor is the length of time the employee stays in the United States. Unlike many other countries, the United States generally does not provide coverage exemptions for Nonresident employees or for employees who have been sent to work within the United States for short periods. For this reason, most foreign workers in the United States are covered under the United States program. If an employer chooses to reimburse an employee for these payroll taxes, the reimbursement is employment compensation subject to income and payroll taxes.

(a) No Internal Revenue Code Exemption

An exemption from Social Security and Medicare taxes applies to Nonresidents who are in the United States in F, J, M, or Q status. This exemption is specific to foreign nationals' immigration status. Therefore, foreign nationals who are in the United States in H-1B status are not entitled to an exemption from Social Security and Medicare taxes under this provision.

H-1B Workers may not work for a sufficiently long enough time in the United States for Social Security benefits to vest. Nevertheless, no claim for a refund of Social Security taxes is available on that basis. However, H-1B Workers who pay Social Security taxes, and who are citizens or lawful residents of a country with which the United States has a social security agreement (described below) may be entitled to a partial benefits under the totalization formula of the agreement.

The primary exception for foreign nationals working in the United States is exemption from U.S. Social Security coverage and taxes (both Social Security and Medicare taxes) under a social security agreement between the foreign national's home country and the United States.

(b) Exemption from Tax under a Social Security Agreement

The United States has social security agreements in force with over 20 countries. Social security agreements have two main purposes. First, they eliminate duplicate social security coverage and taxes on the same covered employment. Second, they help fill gaps in benefit coverage for workers who have divided their careers between the United States and another country (thus the name "totalization" agreements because they also provide benefits by combining total work periods in each applicable country for vesting purposes under each country's applicable vesting rules).

The goal of all U.S. totalization treaties is to eliminate dual social security coverage and taxation while maintaining the coverage of as many workers as possible under the system of the country where they are likely to have the greatest attachment, both while working and after retirement. However, the totalization agreements do not allow dually covered workers or their employers to elect the system to which they will contribute. Also, the agreements do not change the basic coverage provisions under U.S. Social Security law. The agreements simply exempt workers from coverage under the system of one country or the other when their work would otherwise be covered under both systems.

The provisions for eliminating dual coverage are similar in all United States agreements. Each one establishes a basic rule that looks to the location of a worker's employment. Under this "territoriality" rule, an employee who would otherwise be covered by both the United States and a foreign system remains subject exclusively to the coverage laws of the country where the employment is performed unless the worker qualifies as a "detached worker."

Detached Worker Rule

Each social security agreement (except the one with Italy) includes an exception to the territoriality rule designed to minimize disruptions in the coverage careers of workers whose employers send them on temporary assignment to the United States. Under this "detached worker" exception, an employee who is temporarily transferred to work for the same employer in another country remains covered only by the country from which the employee has been sent.

The detached worker rule in United States agreements generally applies to employees whose assignments in the United States are expected to last five years or less. There are exceptions and extensions available in some cases. Exceptions allowing for extension beyond five years must be agreed to by both countries and are generally allowed infrequently and only in compelling cases.

Detached workers and their foreign employers must continue to pay mandatory social security contributions into the foreign system for exemption from U.S. Social Security and Medicare taxes. Payment of voluntary contributions into the foreign plan by foreign nationals, which is allowed by the social security rules of some countries (such as Italy and the U.K.), supports social security coverage for purposes of the agreements with those countries.

Certificates of Coverage

Workers who are exempt from United States coverage under an agreement must document their exemption by obtaining a certificate of coverage from the country that will continue to cover them.

No particular form is required for requesting the certificate. The letter requesting the certificate must include the following information:

- Name of employee
- Date and place of birth
- Marital status
- Citizenship
- Country of lawful permanent residence
- Social security number in both countries if available
- Employer's name and address in both countries
- Place and date of hire
- Beginning and anticipated ending date of assignment

The request must be from the foreign employer that will be maintaining the foreign coverage. Employees with voluntary foreign coverage may also request a Certificate of Coverage.

When the other country issues a certificate certifying that the employee is covered by the foreign system, the U.S. employer does not have to withhold nor submit Social Security and Medicare taxes. The certificates of coverage need be retained only in the employee's files. Under U.S. tax rules, the foreign certificate serves as proof of the exemption from U.S. Social Security and Medicare taxes for the period covered by the certificate.

(Refer to Chapter 11, "Resources," for where to find the agreements and where to obtain a Certificate of Coverage.)

(c) Exemption from Tax under an Income Tax Treaty

The taxes covered by income tax treaties are defined by the Taxes Covered Article of each treaty. Generally, treaties negotiated or modified by protocols since the mid-1980s include a statement that social security taxes or employment taxes are not covered by the treaty. This is consistent with long-standing IRS revenue rulings excluding Social Security taxes from exemption under treaties. (See Rev. Rul. 56-609, *1956-2 C.B. 1066* and Rev. Rul. 66-77, *1966-1 C.B. 242*.)

One treaty, the treaty with the Former USSR, which covers the Newly Independent States (NIS), that have not negotiated a treaty with the United States, includes a broader definition of taxes covered. Under this treaty, the employees are exempt from Social Security and Medicare taxes if their income is exempt from tax under one of the treaty articles. The treaty does not cover the employers' share of Social Security and Medicare taxes because they are excise taxes not income taxes. Because automated payroll systems cannot handle such exemptions, employees must claim Social Security and Medicare tax refunds using claim Form 843. (Refer to IRS Publication 519, *U.S. Tax Guide for Aliens*, for procedures to follow to obtain such refunds.)

8.5 State Income Taxes

The rules for determining income, deductions, and the tax rates vary by state. The rules for determining residency for state income tax purposes are different from the federal rules described in this chapter and also vary by state. As explained in Chapter 7, "State Income Taxes," a foreign national's state tax status may be different from the foreign national's federal tax status.

Each state that imposes income taxes on Residents and Nonresidents has its own rules regarding accessible income and allowable deductions. For information on a particular state's income tax rules, refer to the state tax authority's web site. Visit www.taxadmin.org for links to the applicable web site.

By the terms of the Taxes Covered Article of each treaty, an exemption from tax under an income tax treaty applies to federal income taxes only. However, an income tax treaty exemption may apply to state income taxes indirectly. Many states define income based on federal taxable income, federal adjusted gross income or the definition of income included in the Internal Revenue Code. In these situations, if the income is exempt from federal income tax under a treaty, the income is also exempt from state income taxes unless the state law requires that the treaty exempt income be taken into account for state tax purposes.

CHAPTER 9
U.S. Tax Returns

Foreign nationals who have compensation for U.S. services must submit U.S. federal, and if applicable, state tax returns. Generally, U.S. tax returns are required even if compensation is exempt from tax under an income tax treaty. Foreign nationals departing the United States may have sailing permit requirements as well.

9.1 Sailing Permit Requirement

Before leaving the United States, departing foreign nationals are required to submit an interim tax return or certificate of compliance to the IRS unless an exception applies. Although these rules have been defined for decades, they have been observed more as the exception than the rule. With the development of an entry/exit system for immigration purposes, departing aliens should anticipate that the IRS will have the means for enforcing compliance with these rules in conjunction with the implementation of such a system.

Under the sailing permit procedures, departing foreign nationals must submit either Form 1040C or Form 2063 to the IRS before leaving the United States. Both forms have a "certificate of compliance" (called a "sailing permit" or "departure permit") section. The sailing permit should be submitted to the IRS at an office in the area of employment or in the area of departure within 30 days of the planned departure. Theoretically, departing foreign nationals may be subject to an income tax examination at the point of departure by an IRS employee. Certificates of compliance, signed by an authorized IRS agent, certifies that foreign nationals have satisfied all U.S. tax obligations according to available information. Foreign nationals are required to pay all taxes due with the Form 1040-C. Foreign nationals who have failed to submit required tax returns and pay prior year's taxes must also pay all taxes due for past years.

Certain foreign nationals who have no taxable income or whose departure will not hinder tax collection may submit Form 2063, which requests certain information but does not include a tax computation. H-1B Workers who submit a letter from their U.S. employer guaranteeing to pay any taxes owed, may submit Form 2063. H-4 dependents are exempt from the sailing permit requirement because they are not authorized to work.

For more information on sailing permits, refer to IRS Publication 519, *U.S. Tax Guide for Aliens*. Submission of Form 1040C or 2063 does not eliminate a taxpayer's obligation to submit their U.S. tax return.

9.2 Federal Tax Return

U.S. federal tax returns that nonimmigrants must submit depend on whether they are Residents, Nonresidents, or Dual-status Taxpayers for the calendar year.

(a) Nonresident Tax Return

Nonresidents for the full calendar year, who have compensation for U.S. services, must submit Form 1040NR or 1040NR-EZ. Nonresidents with other U.S. derived income such as dividends or taxable gains must use Form 1040NR and include this income in the return as well, even if the correct amount has been withheld on the income.

Nonresidents who make a first-year choice election (under the rules described in Chapter 3, "Residency start and Termination Dates") must submit a dual status tax return (described below). Married Nonresidents who are part-year Residents based on a first-year choice election may then make a full-year election with their spouse and submit a Form 1040 as a full-year Resident.

Foreign nationals who are Residents under the 183-day residency formula, and who are physically present in the United States for less than 183 days in the calendar year, may submit a Form 1040NR or Form 1040NR-EZ if they qualify for the closer connection exception (explained in Chapter 2, "U.S. Tax Residency Rules"). To submit a Nonresident return using the closer connection exception, they must submit Form 8840 explaining the facts supporting the exception with the return. Such Nonresidents who have no U.S. derived income must submit a signed Form 8840 by June 15. Deductions can be denied on Nonresident tax returns filed more than 16 months past the due date of the return.

For information on Forms 1040NR and 1040NR-EZ, refer to the instructions for the forms and to IRS Publication 519, *U.S. Tax Guide for Aliens*.

(b) Resident Tax Return

Foreign nationals who are Residents for the full calendar year must submit Form 1040 or 1040-EZ tax returns including worldwide income and claiming worldwide deductions for expenses paid from January 1 through December 31.

Foreign nationals making an election to file jointly with a U.S. Citizen or Resident spouse must include their worldwide income from January 1 through December 31. They may claim deductions for worldwide expenses paid in the calendar year. Electing Residents must attach a signed election form to the tax return. For rules on suspending the election in a subsequent year, refer to IRS Publication 519, *U.S. Tax Guide for Aliens*.

For information on the tax rules for Form 1040 refer to the IRS instruction book for filers of Form 1040. (Refer to Chapter 5, "Federal Income Tax Rules for a discussion of the rules for reporting income from outside the United States, and for determining gains on sales of foreign currency denominated assets.)

(c) Dual Status Tax Return

Foreign nationals who are in any one of the following situations must submit a dual status tax return:

- They became Residents during the calendar year under the 183-day residency formula but were not physically present in the United States on January 1.
- They became Residents during the year under the 183-day residency rule, and were physically present in the United States on January 1, but are eligible to be treated as Nonresidents under a treaty residency tie-breaker rule for the part of the year prior to relocation to the United States.
- They are Nonresidents for the calendar year but make the first-year choice election to take advantage of deductions and exemptions available only to Citizens and Residents.
- They departed from the United States in the calendar year, and are deemed to be Residents through December 31, but they claim an earlier residency termination date under the closer connection exception.
- They departed from the United States in the calendar year, and are deemed to be Residents through December 31, but they claim an earlier residency termination date under a tax treaty residency tie-breaker rule.

Residents at the end of the calendar year submit Form 1040 with Form 1040NR as the attached statement. Nonresidents at the end of the calendar year submit Form 1040NR with Form 1040 as the attached statement.

Dual status taxpayers who are married who do not elect to submit a full-year return must compute their tax using married filing separately rates. Spouses who also have U.S. derived income must submit a separate dual status tax return.

Part-year Residents can claim personal exemptions for a spouse (who does not submit a U.S. tax return) and dependents who make part-year resident election and who have either an SSN or ITIN. Election forms for the spouse and dependents must be attached to the tax return. Personal exemptions for qualifying dependents cannot exceed the income reported in the residency period.

Preparation of a dual status tax return is a three-step process.

Determination of Income and Expenses by Period

Income and deductions must be determined based on tax rules that apply for the period – Resident or Nonresident. Income for the nonresidency period is included on a Form 1040NR. Income for the residency period is included on a Form 1040.

Consolidation of Income and Expenses

Net income after deductions subject to graduated rates must be consolidated on the return so that the combined net income after deductions is taxed at the appropriate marginal tax rate. Nonresidents at the end of the year 1) must include residency period income must with the effectively connected income (ECI) and 2) allowable deductions from the residency period must be added to the nonresidency period deductions on Schedule A, *Itemized Deductions*.

Determination of the Tax

The determination of the total tax is a three-step process: 1) the tax using graduated rates is computed on the net income for the combined residency period income and nonresidency ECI and 2) the tax on gross FDAP income is computed separately and 3) the two taxes are totaled on page 2 of the return. Other applicable taxes such as the alternative minimum tax must also be added to the total tax.

For more information about these returns, refer to IRS Publication 519, *U.S. Tax Guide for Aliens*.

9.3 Treaty Claims

The type of U.S. federal tax return on which foreign nationals claim tax treaty benefits depends on whether foreign nationals are Nonresident, Residents, or dual Residents.

(a) Nonresidents

Nonresidents claim tax treaty benefits on Form 1040NR or 1040NR-EZ. They must explain the treaty country and article under which benefits are claimed on the questionnaire page of the form.

Nonresidents who have not remained Residents of the treaty country lose eligibility for most treaty claims (dividends, interest, rents, royalties, etc.) because treaty country residency is required throughout the period of the claim.

(b) Dual Residents

Foreign nationals who have become Residents may be eligible to claim tax treaty benefits under the Teacher and Researcher Article of the treaty using a Saving Clause exception. There are two situations in which Residents claiming tax treaty benefits must submit Form 1040:

- They are dual Residents (i.e. a resident of both the United States and the treaty country), but their facts and circumstances do not support a claim of nonresidency for U.S. tax purposes under the applicable treaty's Residency Article tie-breaker rule.
- They have not remained tax resident in the treaty country for the period for which the tax treaty claim is being made, (i.e. is not a Dual Resident) and, therefore, are not entitled to use the Residency Article tie-breaker rule to support a claim of nonresidency for U.S. tax purposes.

Foreign nationals who are dual Residents claiming nonresidency status under an applicable treaty's Residency Article tie-breaker rule must submit Form 1040NR or Form 1040NR-EZ with a statement or Form 8833 explaining the facts supporting the nonresidency status and the treaty claim.

Residents claim treaty benefits under a Saving Clause exception on a Form 1040 using the following steps:

- Report worldwide income on the return.
- If the income is reported on a Form W-2 or Form 1042-S, report the income on the appropriate line of the return (for example, line 7 in the case of wages or salaries). This allows the income to be matched correctly by the IRS's document match program.
- If the income is reported, record the treaty exempt income on line 21 (Other Income) as a negative using parentheses. Next to the amount write "Exempt Income" and give the treaty country and treaty article. This amount reduces the income to arrive at total income after the treaty exempt amount on line 22.

- Claim the standard deduction, any and all personal exemptions and credits to which Residents are entitled.
- Attach a statement to explain the treaty benefit being claimed as well as the reliance on an exception to the Saving Clause of a treaty in order to qualify for the treaty benefit. (Form 8833 may be used for this purpose although it is not required.)
- Show the computation of the tax when the treaty benefit reduces but does not eliminate the taxable income and record the tax on line 60. Write "Tax from attached statement" beside the amount.
- Submit the Form 1040 to the Philadelphia Service Center.

Although the IRS routinely accepts treaty claims filed under these procedures, occasionally the Service Center rejects a claim because the reviewer lacks familiarity with the Saving Clause exceptions. A Resident submitting a treaty claim that is incorrectly rejected by the IRS may resend the return to the IRS including a copy of the Publication 519 instructions or may seek assistance from the Taxpayer Advocate's Office.

9.4 State Tax Returns

Foreign nationals with compensation subject to state income tax may also be required to submit a state tax return. Whether the tax return must be submitted as a Resident or a Nonresident tax return depends on the state's tax rules.

For information on state tax requirements visit the applicable state tax authority website which can be linked to from www.taxadmin.org.

CHAPTER 10
Individual Taxpayer Identification Numbers

The federal tax laws require foreign nationals with U.S. income regardless of immigration status to include a U.S. taxpayer identification number (TIN) on a U.S. tax return. TINs are also requested by payers for reporting documents. Foreign tax identification numbers cannot be used on these forms. Many U.S. businesses that must routinely report information to the U.S. government, such as banks, investment houses, and pension administrators, also require a TIN from their customers, whether or not the customers' income is required to be reported. In addition, many federal, state, and local agencies require a TIN for identification purposes. For example, state motor vehicle registries require a TIN on an application for a U.S. driver's license.

Only foreign nationals who are work authorized are eligible to obtain a U.S. Social Security number (SSN). The IRS introduced the ITIN in 1996 to provide foreign nationals who are not eligible for Social Security numbers (SSNs) with a means to comply with the tax laws. An ITIN is a nine-digit tax identification number (TIN) issued by the IRS. The number always begins with the number 9 and has a 7 or 8 in the fourth digit, for example 9XX-7X-XXX. Therefore, foreign nationals who are not work authorized, who are required to have an ITIN for tax reasons (such as being claimed as a dependent on a U.S. tax return), must obtain an ITIN from the IRS. Once acquired, this ITIN can be used for other purposes. Under new ITIN application procedures introduced for 2004, the timing of obtaining an ITIN may be problematic for foreign nationals required to have a TIN for other purposes, such as driver's license.

10.1 Individuals Eligible for ITINs

The following foreign nationals, who are not eligible to apply for an SSN, must apply for an ITIN:

   a. Nonresidents eligible to obtain the benefit of reduced withholding under an income tax treaty
   b. Nonresidents who are required to file a U.S. tax return or who are filing a U.S. tax return only to claim a refund
   c. U.S. Residents (based on the 183-day tax residency formula) who are required to file a U.S. tax return

d. Aliens eligible to be claimed as dependents by U.S. Citizens or Residents on a U.S. Form 1040 tax return

e. Spouses of U.S. Citizens or Residents who can be claimed as dependents or who elect to file a joint U.S. tax return with spouses who are U.S. Citizens or Residents

f. Nonresident students, professors, or researchers who are required to file a U.S. tax return

g. Dependents or spouses of Nonresidents who can be claimed as dependents on a Form 1040NR Nonresident tax return

The letters correspond to the category letters on Form W-7, *Application for IRS Individual Taxpayer Identification Number*.

10.2 Documentation Requirements

The documents that substantiate the information provided on a Form W-7 include a valid foreign passport. The passport information, such as the name, date of birth, and country of citizenship, must be the same as the information provided on Form W-7.

If a foreign national does not submit a valid foreign passport, the foreign national must provide at least two or more of the following documents that are current and that verify identity with a name and photograph, and support the foreign national's claim of foreign status.

- National identification card that shows a photo, name, current address, date of birth, and expiration date
- U.S. driver's license
- Civil birth certificate
- Foreign driver's license
- U.S. state identification card
- Foreign voter's registration card
- U.S. military identification card
- Foreign military identification card
- U.S. visa issued by the U.S. Department of State
- U.S. Citizenship and Immigration Services (USCIS) photo identification
- Medical records (limited to dependents)
- School records (limited to dependents and students)

The Form W-7 instructions state that foreign nationals may send original documents with the form, and they will be returned to the foreign nationals. This is not a wise choice. Instead, foreign nationals can submit copies of documents that are certified by the issuing agency or official custodian of the original record, a difficult if not impossible choice.

Documents can be notarized by U.S. notaries, legally authorized within their local jurisdiction to certify that the document is a true copy of the original. To do this, notaries must see the valid, unaltered, original document and verify that the copy conforms to the original. The instructions note that notaries are available at U.S. embassies and consulates worldwide. Dealing with notaries at embassies and consulates can be an expensive and time-consuming process, and inconvenient for foreign nationals who do not live near a city with an embassy or consulate. Foreign notaries are acceptable as outlined by the Hague Convention. (Form information on the latter, go to the IRS website at www.irs.gov and search on "Hague Convention." Not all countries are signatories of the Convention, however.)

The IRS website, which includes reference to the new ITIN application procedures, states that assistance with ITIN applications is available at IRS Taxpayer Assistance Centers (TACs) in the United States on a walk-in or appointment basis. The IRS will notarize documents for the applicants. The website also notes that applicants outside the United States may contact an overseas IRS office to find out if that office accepts Form W-7 applications. However, there are now only three offices — Frankfurt, London, and Paris.

10.3 Application Submission Procedures

The IRS now accepts Form W-7, ITIN applications only accepted for a tax administration purpose. Therefore, taxpayers in general are now required to submit Form W-7 with, *and not in advance of,* the submission of their original, completed tax returns for which the ITIN is needed unless an exception applies.

(a) Submissions with Tax Returns

The Form W-7 instructions specify that applicants who check boxes b, c, d, e, or g (see page 69) must submit Form W-7 with their completed tax return. This is the case even if the ITIN is for a spouse or dependent. If the tax return requires more than one ITIN for the same return (such as for a spouse and other dependents), all Forms W-7 must be attached to the same return. No separate filing of the tax return is required. This application procedure is obviously problematic for filing state income tax returns which also require a TIN, since taxpayers may not have an ITIN until long after the filing deadline for state returns. To minimize such problems, taxpayers should file their federal tax returns as early as possible.

The tax return with the Form W-7 must *not* be submitted to the address specified in the instructions to the tax return. Rather, the taxpayer must submit the tax return, with the Form W-7 attached to the front of the return (including the documentation attached to Form W-7 which supports the ITIN application) to the following address:

> Internal Revenue Service
> Philadelphia Service Center
> ITIN Unit
> P.O. Box 447
> Bensalem, PA 19020

The instructions state that taxpayers are responsible for submitting original, completed tax returns with Forms W-7 by the due date applicable to the tax return, generally April 15 of the year following the calendar year covered by the tax return. (Nonresident aliens who have no income subject to wage withholding have a June 15 due date for the Form 1040NR or 1040NR-EZ tax return.)

(b) Tax Return Extensions

The instructions state that foreign nationals submitting an extension of time to file using Form 4868 or Form 2688 or making an estimated tax payment using Form 1040-ES or 1040-ES(NR) should not file Form W-7 with these forms. Rather, the foreign nationals should write "ITIN TO BE REQUESTED" wherever an SSN or ITIN is requested.

As a general rule, it is not a good practice to send forms to the IRS that lack a TIN. This is especially the case when foreign nationals must submit a payment with a form, such as a payment with an extension, or an estimated payment. Also, in order to assure that a payment is credited to an foreign national's account, the SSN or ITIN must appear on the check submitted with the form. In situations in which taxpayers must submit a form and check without an SSN or ITIN, taxpayers should send the form and check certified mail, return receipt requested, and obtain a copy of the cancelled check from the bank. Foreign nationals should always keep copies of forms, checks, and other information sent to the IRS.

(c) Exceptions to the Tax Return Submission Procedures

The Form W-7 instructions explain four exceptions to the requirement that a completed tax return be filed with the Form W-7.

- Passive income — treaty benefits (box "a") or third party withholding
- Other income (wages, salary, compensation) — treaty benefits (box "a") or foreign students receiving scholarships or fellowships (box "f")
- Third party reporting-mortgage interest (box "h")
- Disposition by foreign persons of U.S. real property interest

Foreign nationals claiming a treaty exemption under Exception 1 or 2 must include the name of the treaty country and the treaty article under which the treaty claim is being made beside box "h" on Form W-7.

For each exception, the instructions specify the type of additional documentation and/or IRS forms that foreign nationals must include with Form W-7 supporting the need for the ITIN; for example:

- Under Exception 1, a partnership interest, a copy of the partnership agreement along with the partnership's EIN
- Under Exception 3, evidence of a home mortgage loan, which could be a commitment letter from the financial institution, a broker's listing agreement, or similar documentation
- Under Exception 4, a copy of Form 8288-B, *Application for Withholding Certificate for Dispositions by Foreign Persons of U.S. Real Property Interests*, and a copy of the contract for the sale

10.4 Acceptance Agents

The IRS permits the use of Acceptance Agents to facilitate the issuance of ITINs. Acceptance Agents are organizations, such as colleges and universities, financial institutions, casinos, and accounting and tax firms, which come into contact with large numbers of foreign nationals requiring ITINs. Acceptance Agents enter into agreements with the IRS regarding their responsibilities to review applicants' documentation and complete certificates of accuracy for submission with Forms W-7. The IRS maintains a list of Acceptance Agents, which is available on the IRS website. Acceptance Agents may charge a fee for this service.

Prior to the issuance of the new Form W-7 instructions, Acceptance Agents forward the certificates and applications directly to the IRS for processing. The ITINs were sent back to the Acceptance Agent who forwarded them to the foreign national applicants. In this manner, the Acceptance Agent had the number needed for withholding and reporting responsibilities. Under the new procedures, submission of Forms W-7 certified by an Acceptance Agent must follow the same procedures as if the foreign nationals submitted the Form W-7 without the assistance of an Acceptance Agent.

10.5 Acceptance Agent Application Procedures

On December 19, 2005, the IRS issued Rev. Proc. 2006-10 providing guidance for qualifying as an Acceptance Agent and executing an agreement with the IRS to facilitate the issuance of certain IRS taxpayer identification numbers (TINs) to foreign nationals and foreign entities. Under Rev. Proc. 2006-10 all existing Acceptance Agent agreements will expire as of December 31, 2006. Therefore, Acceptance Agents subject to the expiring agreements must reapply to retain their Acceptance Agent status.

The new Acceptance Agent application is a three-step process:

1) Submission of an application to become an Acceptance Agent (Form 13551)

2) Determination by the IRS of the suitability of the applicant to become an Acceptance Agent

3) Negotiation of an applicable Acceptance Agent agreement with the IRS

Refer to Rev. Proc 2006-10 for details regarding the application process.

CHAPTER 11
Resources

11.1 Websites

The Internal Revenue Service (IRS) Website, www.irs.gov

The IRS's website provides a wealth of information for U.S. taxpayers and their employers and payers. Included on the website are IRS forms and publications that can be printed out or saved. Prior forms as well as current forms are available.

The website includes extensive discussions about the tax rules and procedures that apply to payments to foreign persons. Many of these discussions are helpful for foreign national taxpayers and their payers.

The site also includes the complete text of income tax treaties. Readers need to check for protocols amending the treaties that follow the treaty texts that were amended. This can be very confusing for treaties with many protocols such as the 1980 treaty with Canada, which has protocols amending parts of treaties amended by earlier protocols.

The Social Security Administration (SSA) Website, www.socialsecurity.gov

The SSA's website provides "Information for Employers" such as "Employer Responsibilities When Hiring Foreign Workers." The *Information for Employers* page also links to instructions for Social Security Number Verification.

The website includes the International Programs page, which provides the social security ("totalization") agreements as well as booklets describing how the agreements work and how to obtain certificates of coverage under the agreements. Also included on the International Programs page is "Your Payments While You Are Outside the United States."

Windstar Technologies, Inc. (Windstar), www.windstar.com

Windstar, known nationally as the leader in international tax and immigration compliance, offers the most up-to-date and cost-effective software products available to navigate the complex challenges of compliance with U.S. tax and immigration rules for payments to foreign workers, scholars, and international visitors.

Windstar's website offers a wealth of free resources including:

Income Tax Treaties

The income tax treaties on Windstar's website are posted for individuals and their employers and payers. They include those treaty articles relevant to foreign nationals living, working, residing in, or visiting the United States. To make the treaties easier for individuals to understand, Windstar:

- Presents articles in the same order for all treaties
- Provides consistent headings for the articles
- Notes whether a treaty article is not included in the treaty
- Provides the name of the country in brackets following the term "Contracting State"
- Includes the protocol paragraphs, which amend or add to the treaty, following the amended article
- Provides comments from the Treasury Explanations of treaties to clarify certain benefits and limitations

Windstar posts information about updates of existing treaties and new treaties as they become effective.

For more information about how tax treaties work refer to *Tax Treaty Benefits for Foreign Nationals Performing U.S. Services* by Paula N. Singer, Esq. published by Windstar Publishing, Inc. available at shopping.windstar.com.

e-Newsletter, A View From the Crow's Nest

Windstar's e-newsletter, *A View from the Crow's Nest* includes a tax or immigration-related topic in each issue, such as:

- Tax Residency Rules
- New Treaty With Japan Poses Challenges for Taxpayers, Administrators, and the IRS
- New Rules for Withholding on Wages of Nonresidents

Individuals can sign up for the *Crow's Nest* on the Windstar website home page. *Crow's Nest* archives are available for free on Windstar's website.

11.2 IRS Publications

Publication 15, *Circular E, Employer's Tax Guide*

This publication explains the tax responsibilities of employers—withholding, depositing, reporting, and paying employment taxes. The publication explains the wage-withholding and employment tax rules and procedures. The publication includes a description of withholding on wages of Nonresidents.

Publication 15-B, *Employer's Tax Guide to Fringe Benefits*, contains information about the employment tax treatment and valuation of various types of non-cash compensation.

Publication 463, *Travel, Entertainment, Gift, and Car Expenses*

This publication describes the rules under which certain travel, food, and lodging expenses may be deducted by taxpayers because they are considered to be ordinary and necessary business-related expenses. Included is a discussion of when taxpayers are away from their "tax home" and entitled to claim these expenses as temporarily-away-from-home business expenses.

This publication also discusses the accountable-plan rules that allow employers and payers to exclude temporarily-away-from-home business expenses from income. These rules are also discussed in Chapter 13 of Publication 535, *Business Expenses*.

See also IRS Publication 1542 *Per Diem Rates (for Travel within the Continental United States)*.

Publication 515, *Withholding of Tax on Nonresident Aliens and Foreign Entities*

This publication is for withholding agents who pay income to foreign persons, including nonresident aliens, foreign corporations, foreign partnerships, foreign trusts, foreign estates, foreign governments, and international organizations.

Included in this publication are descriptions of the persons responsible for withholding (called "withholding agents"), the types of income subject to withholding, and the information-return and tax-return filing obligations of withholding agents, and their tax-deposit requirements. The publication also discusses the rules that apply generally to payments of U.S. source income to foreign persons. Also included in this publication are discussions of the special rules that apply to dispositions of U.S. real estate by foreign persons and withholding of partnerships with ECI.

Because this publication attempts to provide advice on all types of payments to all types of foreign persons, it can be confusing for nontax specialists who do not deal with many of the payments discussed in this publication.

Publication 517, *Moving Expenses*

This publication explains the deduction of certain expenses of moving to a new location when the taxpayer's tax home has changed to the new location. It discusses taxpayers who are eligible for deductions, expenses that are deductible and those that are not, and how employer reimbursements impact the deductions.

Publication 519, *U.S. Tax Guide for Aliens*

This publication is primarily for aliens who have U.S. tax-return filing obligations. Most of the rules discussed are for aliens who are nonresidents since residents are generally taxed in the same manner as U.S. Citizens.

Included are discussions and helpful charts about how to determine tax residency status--Resident, Nonresident, or Dual-status, the source of income rules for various types of income, special exclusions from income, how the income is taxed, and tax-return filing obligations.

This publication also includes overviews of income tax treaty benefits for students, trainees, professors, teachers, and researchers, and for foreign nationals receiving self-employment or employment compensation. The certifications required for Form 8233 are included in this publication, but only for those treaties that became effective prior to 1994.

Publication 901, *U.S. Tax Treaties*

This publication provides an overview of the benefits and limitations of the treaties. It includes two tables providing an overview of treaty rates and benefits:

- Table 1: Tax Rates on Income Other Than Personal Service Income Under Chapter 3, Internal Revenue Code and Income Tax Treaties
- Table 2: Compensation for Personal Services Performed in the United States Exempt from U.S. Income Tax Under Tax Treaties

The IRS cautions readers that this publication should only be used as a quick reference. It is not a complete guide to all provisions of every income tax treaty. For example, provisions discussed in Chapter 6, "Income Tax Treaty Benefits," such as the residency requirements, saving clause and ex ceptions, and IRS policy requiring reestablishment of treaty-country residency between treaty claims are not addressed in this publication.

Other Helpful Publications

- Publication 54, *Tax Guide for U.S. Citizens and Resident Aliens Abroad,*
- Publication 514, *Foreign Tax Credits for Individuals*
- Publication 1546, *The Taxpayer Advocate Service —How to Get Help with Unresolved Tax Problems,*
- Publication 1586, *Reasonable Cause Regulations and Requirements for Missing and Incorrect Name/TINs,* and
- Publication 1915, *Understanding Your IRS Individual Taxpayer Identification Number*

Index

10-day *de minimis* rule, 9
183-day residency formula, 5
   change of status, 19
   closer connection exception to, 7
   days not counted in, 6
Acceptance Agents, 73
Additional withholding amount, 53
Anti-avoidance rule, 16
Article(s). *See also* Teacher/Researcher Article(s)
   Residency, 7
   successive, claims, 39, 40
   Taxes Covered, 61
Asset sales in foreign currency, 26
Associated hospital, Teacher/Researcher Article requirement for, 35
Automobiles
   cents per mile alternative, 51
   company provided, 50
   reportable value, 50
   values of leased, 50
   values of owned, 50
Avoidance of double taxation, 27
Back-to-back limitations, 40
Benefit(s)
   back-to-back, limitations, 40
   combined periods of, 40
   loss of, 32
   one-time use limitation, 39
   period limitation for teachers and researchers, 36
   prospective loss of, 37
   public, requirement, 41
   retroactive loss of, 38
   successive treaty article claims for, 39

Cars. *See* Automobiles
Certificate(s)
   of coverage under social security agreements, 60
   of coverage, letter to request, 60
   of foreign status, 31
Change of status, 19
   from F-1 or J-1 student to H-1B, 20
   from J-1 non-student to H-1B, 19
   under 183-day residency formula, 19
Claims. *See* Treaty claims
Closer connection exception, 7
   residency termination date, 14
Combined benefit periods, 40
Compensation. *See also* Income
   services vs. scholarship or fellowship, 41
   teacher and researcher, 33, 36
   treaty exempt, 55
Consecutive dual-status year rule, 15
Currency translation rules, 25
Days not counted, 6
Deduction(s)
   company-provided automobile, 50
   immigration fees, 53
   moving expenses, 51
   pension plan contribution, 52
   per diem, 49
   relocation, 47
   tax return preparation fees, 52
   temporarily away from home, 47
Departure permits, 63
Dependent H-4 work authorization, 2
Detached worker rule, 60
Domicile rules, state, 44

Double taxation, avoidance of, 27
Dual-residency treaty claims, 67
Dual-status
  consecutive-year rule, 15
  tax returns, 65
  taxpayer tax rule, 28
ECI, 23
Educational institution,
    Teacher/Researcher Article
    requirement for, 34
Effectively connected income, 23, 24
Election(s)
  first-year choice, 11
  full-year residency, 13, 55
  residency, 11
  wage withholding, 14, 55
Employment compensation, tax
    exemptions from, 32
Exception(s)
  closer connection, 7, 14
Exemption(s)
  employment compensation, 32
  income tax treaty, 31
  loss of benefits, 32
  Medicare taxes, 58
  pre-location visits, 32
  Social Security, 58
  state tax, 44, 61
  teacher and researcher compensation, 33
  treaty, for compensation, 55
  U.S. source FDAP income, 31
  under social security agreements, 59
Expatriate payrolls, 47
FDAP income, 23, 31
Federal income tax rules, 23
Federal tax return, 55
  See also Tax return(s)
Fellowship or scholarship vs. services, 41
First-year choice election, 11
Foreign income
  for foreign operations, 28
  from account interest, 28
  from rental of real estate, 26

Foreign tax credits, 27
Form(s)
  1040-C, 63
  1042, 57
  1042-S, 57
  1116, 27
  2063, 63
  5471, 29
  8233, 55
  8833, 8
  8840, 7
  DS-230, 7
  ETA-750, 7
  ETA-9089, 7
  I-130, 7
  I-140, 7
  I-485, 7
  I-508, 7
  I-94, 2
  part-year residency election, 13
  TD 90-22.1, 28
  W-2, 2, 47, 57
  W-4, 54
  W-7, 3
  W-8BEN, 24
  W-9 U.S. person treaty claim
      attachment, 56
Full-year residency election, 13
  withholding rules, 55
Guidelines, expatriate payroll, 47
H-1B specialty worker
  Social Security number for, 2
  spouse of, 2
  work authorization, 1
Hospital, Teacher/Researcher Article
    requirement for associated, 35
Immigration fees, deducting, 53
Income. *See also* Compensation
  effectively connected, 24
  employment, treaty exemptions from, 31
  exemptions, 31
  FDAP, 23
  foreign real estate rental, 26
  from foreign corporation, for foreign
      operation, 28

Index

interest, from foreign accounts, 28
sale of assets in foreign currency, 65
stock ownership in foreign
    corporation, 28
U.S. source, 23
Income tax treaty exemptions. *See*
    Exemption(s)
Interest income, foreign account, 28
ITIN(s)
    dependent, 3
    treaty exemption requirement of, 57
Lawful permanent resident(s)
    becoming a, 7
    state tax rules for, 43
Limitation(s)
    back-to-back limitations, 40
    benefit period, teacher and researcher, 36
    combined benefit periods, 40
    one-time use, 39
    prospective loss of benefits, 37
    retroactive loss of benefits, 38
    subsequent-year residency, 15
Loss of treaty benefits, 32
LPR(s)
    becoming a, 7
    state tax rules for, 43
Medical school, Teacher/Researcher
    Article requirement for, 35
Medicare tax exemptions, 58
Moving expenses, deducting, 51
Nonresident(s)
    claiming status as, 5, 7
    income of, subject to U.S. tax, 23
    special withholding rules for, 53
    tie-breaker rule for, status, 7
    treaty claims, 67
One-time use benefit, 39
One-year rule, 48
Payrolls, expatriate, 47
Pension plan contribution, deducting, 52
Per diem amounts, deducting, 49
Permanent home, 7
Pre-relocation visits, 32

Principle residence, sale of, 26
Prospective loss of benefits, 37
Public benefit requirement, 41
Publications, IRS, 77
Quijano rule, 26, 27
Relocation
    deductible moving expenses for, 51
    deductions, 47
    visits to U.S. prior to, 32
Rental income, foreign real estate, 26
Research institution, Teacher/Researcher
    Article requirement for, 34
Research scholars
    scholarship compensation for, 41
    services compensation for, 41
    special considerations for, 41
Residence, sale of principle, 26
Residency
    183-day formula for, 5
    closer connection exception to, 7
    determining status of tax, 5
    elections, 11
    establishing permanent, 7
    first-year choice election for, 11
    full-year elections for, 13
    lawful permanent resident, 7
    state tax requirements for, 43
    tie-breaker rule for, 7
    wage-withholding election, 14, 55
Residency Article, 7
    See also Residency
Residency start date, 9
    10-day *de minimis* rule for, 9
    establishing a later, 9
    tie-breaker rule to determine, 10
    withholding rules and, 54
Residency termination date, 9, 14
    anti-avoidance rule, 16
    closer connection exception, 14
    consecutive dual-status year rule, 15
    establishing a later, 15
    tie-breaker rule to determine, 17
    while on assignment abroad, 17
Retroactive loss of benefits, 38

Rule(s)
    10-day *de minimis*, 9
    anti-avoidance, 16
    assets sold in foreign currency, 26
    consecutive dual-status year, 15
    currency translation, 25
    detached worker, 60
    disclosing foreign accounts, 28
    double taxation avoidance, 27
    dual-status taxpayer, 28
    effectively connected income, 24
    federal income tax, 23
    foreign corporation stock ownership, 28
    foreign real estate rental income, 26
    forward attribution, 51
    nonresident tax, 23
    one-year, 48
    principle residence sale, 26
    Quijano, 26, 27
    special withholding, 53
    state tax, 43
    stock ownership in foreign corporation, 28
    tax, for residents, 25
    tie-breaker, 7, 17
    withholding, 47
Sailing permits, 63
Sale of assets in foreign currency, 26
Saving Clause, 31
Scholarship or fellowship vs. services, 41
Social security agreements, 59
    certificate of coverage under, 60
    detached worker rule, 60
Social Security number. *See* SSN(s), ITIN(s), TIN(s)
Social Security tax exemption, 58
Spouse
    H-4 derivative status, work authorization for, 2
    withholding rules for, 53
SSN(s)
    delayed issuance of, 2
    obtaining a, 2
    treaty exemption requirement of, 57

Start date, residency, 9
    10-day *de minimis* rule for, 9
    establishing a later, 9
    tie-breaker rule to determine, 10
    withholding rules and, 54
State taxes
    deductions from, 44, 61
    domicile rule for, 44
    residence requirement for, 44
    rules for, 43, 44, 61
    treaty exemptions for, 44
Status change, 19
    from F-1 or J-1 student to H-1B, 20
    from J-1 non-student to H-1B, 19
    under 183-day residency formula, 19
Stock ownership in foreign corporation, income from, 28
Student/Trainee Article(s)
    back-to-back limitations, 40
    combined benefit period, 40
Subsequent-year residency limitation, 15
Successive treaty article claims, 39
Tax exemptions. *See* Exemption(s)
Tax home, 48
    determining, 5
Tax residency rules, 5
Tax return(s)
    deducting preparation fees, 52
    departing foreign national, 63
    dual-status, 65
    federal, 64
    foreign national resident, 64
    nonresident federal, 64
    sailing permit, documentation for, 63
Tax rules, 25,
    See also Rule(s)
Taxes Covered Articles, 61
Taxpayer Identification Number. *See* TIN(s)
Teacher/Researcher Article(s). *See also* Research scholars
    associated hospital requirement, 35
    back-to-back limitations, 40

Index

benefit period limitations, 36
claims for successive, 39
combined benefit period, 40
compensation exemptions, 33
educational institution requirement, 34
institution requirement, 34
limitations, 36
medical school requirement, 35
one-time use limitation, 39
prospective loss of benefits, 37
public benefit requirement, 41
research institution requirement, 34
retroactive loss of benefits, 38
Saving Clause, 31

Temporarily away-from-home
deductible expense, 47
expense deductions when, 49
per diem deductions, 49
per diem deductions when, 49

Termination date, residency, 9, 14
anti-avoidance rule, 16
closer connection exception, 14
consecutive dual-status year rule, 15
establishing a later, 15
tie-breaker rule to determine, 17
while on assignment abroad, 17

Tie-breaker rules
residency start date determined with, 10
residency termination date determined with, 17

TIN(s)
obtaining, 2
treaty exemption requirement of, 57

Totalization agreements, 59
certificate of coverage under, 60
detached worker rule, 60

Treaty benefits. *See* Benefit(s)

Treaty claims, 66
dual resident, 67
nonresident, 67

U.S. source income, 23

U.S. tax residency rules. *See* Tax residency rules

U.S. tax returns. *See* Tax return(s)

Visits to U.S. before relocating, 32

Wage withholding
special rules for nonresident, 53
temporarily away-from-home, 47

Wages. *See* Compensation; Income

Wage-withholding elections, 14

Websites
list of useful sites, 75

Windstar Technologies
resources available, 75

Withholding rules, 47
full-year residency election, 55
residency start date, 54

Work authorization, 1
dependent, 2
Form I-94, 2
spouse, 2